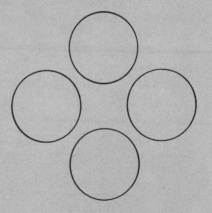

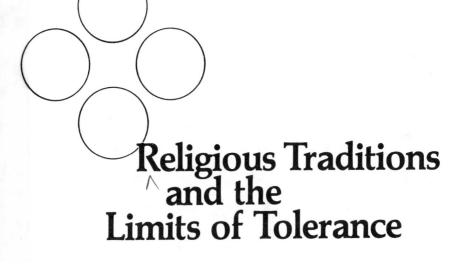

Religious Traditions and the Limits of Tolerance

Louis J. Hammann

and Harry M. Buck

Editors

With Michael McTighe

ANIMA BOOKS

LIBRARY OF CONGRESS
Library of Congress Cataloging-in-Publication Data

Religious traditions and the limits of tolerance / Louis J. Hammann
and Harry M. Buck, editors, with Michael McTighe.
    x,158 p. 22 cm.
    ISBN 0-89012-047-1
    1. Religions. 2. Religious tolerance. I. Hammann, Louis J.,
1929-   . II. Buck, Harry Merwyn. III. McTighe, Michael J.,
1948- .
BL85.R39 1988
291.1'72 — dc19   88-2441
                                          CIP

Anima Publications is a subdivision of Conococheague Associates, Inc.,
1053 Wilson Avenue, Chambersburg, Pennsylvania 17201. Printed in USA.

Contents

Celebrating the Human Experience

Circles That Interconnect

The colloquy from which this volume emerged was made possible by a generous grant from the Pennsylvania Humanities Council. The colloquy, sponsored by Gettysburg College and Wilson College, was held in the spring of 1987.

Circles That Include
and
Circles That Exclude

The human community is a fragile construct
indeed. In how many ways can it be broken
and divided against itself?

1

The Limits of Tolerance

Louis J. Hammann

Most of us live in religious isolation. It seems we know very little
about the beliefs, practices, or experiences of others who are involved in religious communities different from our own. The reasons for such a condition are, I am sure, legion. The fact is singular.
Most of us are reluctant to extend the courtesy of understanding to
those on other paths. We prefer to act as though the interstate high-
way that we follow is the only one with a significant destination.

Still, most seriously religious persons are likely to admit that
tolerance is a virtue. The virtue may lose its shine, however, when
we begin to compare our own persuasions to those belonging to
people of whom we have been tolerant. Then we may retreat to a
defensive position where we begin to protect ourselves by attacking
or at least belittling others.

It is the ignorance of isolation, then, that may tempt us to be
tolerant. On the other hand, the desire to understand may discover
for us unsuspected differences that strain credulity and threaten
our previously safe identity. We face here a serious dilemma.

Even if understanding is a moral good, as it surely is, it can still
lead to a failure of good will within the human community. Tolerance, on the other hand, even though an acknowledged virtue,

may rest on ignorance that can hardly be called moral in any ordinary sense of the word.

The uncertainties attached to religious tolerance, however, are even more intricate than we have thought so far. For example, the very notion of "tolerance" is itself not unequivocal, even if tolerant behavior is a virtue. I would argue that there are "modalities" of religious tolerance that further obscure the status of the virtue. We can be tolerant along a spectrum that ranges from affirming others as an honest invitation to dialogue to hesitant acquiescence that may imperfectly cover up disdain slipping precariously into hostility. But more of the ambiguities and dilemmas later.

One thing is certain: The human community is a fragile construct indeed. In how many ways can it be broken and divided against itself? The question is rhetorical, of course, since no one would presume actually to count the ways. Still, the opportunities for intolerance and hostility that plague the human species have elicited remarkable ingenuity among us. On the intra-human level, variations of gender, color, ethnicity, age, size, and intelligence inflict upon each of us suspicion of others. Class, nationality, and religion are some of the gross differences that turn us against each other. Tolerance, it seems, is not one of our *spontaneous* virtues. But there is a paradox.

The divine presence loves what it has created. Thereby, love becomes a virtue of the divine and so a divine virtue. Surely, ordinary piety should do no less than imitate that virtue. Human beings, overwhelmed by absolute love, must find it in themselves to love one another, even in face of the differences that divide and distinguish them from each other. The divine itself, after all, must be able to "see beyond" the mere humanity it has created. It must be able to override the virtually endless diversity that distinguishes the human order.

On the other hand, however, we seem unable or unwilling to practice the virtue that we attribute to the divine. Though God "bears" us, we do not find it in our human selves to bear each other as happy burdens. That, after all, is what "tolerance" implies. The word is derived from the Latin verb that means to pick up, to carry some object. Presumably, under divine command, or doing what the truth demands, we should gladly "bear the burden" of human variety, but we do not, without at least some reservation, without begrudging the differences that create the marvelous kaleidiscope of humanity. Tolerance has its limits.

The paradox is disarming. By a strange logic that scrambles the universal and the particular, as well as divine virtue and merely human morality, our inclusive vision excludes. Secure in our parochial versions of the truth of universal love, we discover intolerance to be the shadow of tolerance; exclusion the reciprocal of inclusion; the insistence on conformity, the reflex of a love that should be able to dissolve differences but often does not. And again we must conclude that tolerance has its limits.

This collection of essays is meant to search for those limits as felt by persons who live within viable religious communities. The first piece is especially sensitive to the dilemma set forth above. It discovers the roots of intolerance in that very community that has itself born the terrible brunt of intolerance through so many centuries. The Jewish claim that there is only one God entails distrust of, even hostility to, those who cannot countenance that claim. Still, those who determine to obey the divine law as though it had been revealed exclusively to them, are eventually chastened when they discern the implications of their own intolerance. The logic of social history becomes clear: Theological arrogance draws abuse to those who practice it. Intolerance perpetuates itself and comes to prey on the intolerant. The rabbis eventually express the logical necessity of religious tolerance when they declare, "God will uproot from the world everyone who hates his fellow man."

God, we suppose, will save us by expunging the animosity that seems to come so naturally to us. Otherwise our humanity would be completely compromised by the self-destructive intolerance that plagues the human spirit.

But even those who are moved by monotheism to despise others, who have missed its presumptive truth, are able to reflect that they had also been victims of intolerance. Torah reminds the Jews, "You shall not oppress a stranger; you know the heart of a stranger, for you were strangers in the land of Egypt" (Exodus 23:9). The Jews have forced themselves to remember what they, with all of us, forget: "The best of us are only human." The "only," here, points beyond the human to a transcendent reality whose best motives are the redemption of the human.

So, again, where are the limits of religious tolerance? Are they coextensive with our humanity? Then surely the limits are narrow and we may not be able to avoid much longer the self-destructive impulses that haunt our personal and communal lives. And if this be the case, then we are trapped in a web of our own devising. But, if religious people are servants of another truth, then the limits are set beyond even our imagining. If that be the case, however, then how shall we know who we are and what we are? For our identity as human beings depends on living within recognizable *limits*.

In practical terms, for many the boundaries that define them are the religious traditions that claim them. What if those very traditions force on them an identity that requires intolerance? The dilemma is acute. What often may bind us to the universe and to each other is the very sense that makes us hostile to each other. We are burdened by the claim that persuades us that we have been especially chosen by the universe to protect the truth that passes understanding.

Hypnotized by that paradox, stunned by that irony, what can we do? What should we do? It was this two edged sword that we asked some of our colleagues to test. Where would they locate the limits of religious tolerance? Did any of them feel constraints on their will to tolerance? Or was "tolerance" only an illusion behind which the particular human person harbored a grudge against vagrant and benighted others?

The first essay in the series allows itself no reprieve from candor. Stanley Rosenbaum "will argue that Judaism is preeminently responsible for the tradition of nationalism and intolerance that bedevils the West unto this day." But this is also the tradition that produced the Talmudist whose human sense of ambiguity often constrained him to affirm, "Both this view and that, too, are the words of the living God."

Are the limits of religious tolerance drawn indelibly for the monotheist and obliterated for the atheist? If we would appreciate

Judaism, we cannot be so categorical. For there and elsewhere we find narrowness and breadth exhibited in the same tradition. But who of us can tolerate the unresolved dilemma forever: It is as adherents of a universal truth that we ourselves are privileged to practice exclusion. Thereby we set the limits of religious tolerance perilously close to the borders of our own egoes.

In his unerring way, Rosenbaum takes us to the center of the issue: "If our particular version of truth is not Truth, then religious faith becomes relative . . . . If it is Truth, how do we accommodate those who hold otherwise?" Rosenbaum concludes, "The dangers of this dilemma are all too apparent." During our inquiry some will argue that intolerance of other religious persuasions is "sinful" Others, however, will argue that religious tolerance compromises the integrity of particular convictions — and hence is no virtue at all. Are we, then, as committed persons damned if we do and damned if we don't? Is the limit of religious tolerance a theological or a psychological question? Must we purchase peace in the body social by giving up the "peace that passes understanding"? Does the intolerance that we impute to other religious folks really reflect our own intolerance embedded in the "habits of our hearts"? The questions proliferate, and we may wonder whether it is God or we who beat our heads against the limits of religious tolerance.

To obtain salvation one need not be
theologically "right," but "righteous."

2

Monotheism and the Roots of Intolerance

Stanley N. Rosenbaum

Between 1933 and 1945 Germany produced an indigestible amount
of nationalism, and the rest of Europe choked on it. But we should
not see this paroxysm as unique. Nationalism has been the besetting
sin of Europe for three hundred years, easily resisting the efforts of
idealists to homogenize it into something more palatable. Before
1914 German and French Socialists pledged not to fight, but when
the guns of August went off they, too, plunged right in.

There are too many factors in this sorry situation for such a short
discussion, but I would suggest that lurking behind the thrones of
Europe has always been that well-known *eminence grise*, religion.
Not capital R religion, to be sure, but national churches, e.g.,
Lutheran Sweden, Orthodox Russia, Catholic France. Europe has
been nominally Christian for a millenium so, as a Jew, I might have
smugly considered myself above the battle, at least until the found-
ing of modern Israel in 1948. Even Zionism, the Jewish nationalism

The author wishes to thank Mary Rosenbaum and Kasey Kesselring for significant con-
tributions to this essay.

of the nineteenth century, was more "the bastard child of European nationalism than the legitimate offspring of Jewish religious aspirations."[1]

However, I cannot exonerate Judaism from unwitting complicity in the modern predicament; just the opposite is the case. Judaism is preeminently responsible for the tradition of nationalism and intolerance that bedevils that West unto this day.

When Israel was young, Assyria, Egypt, and Hitti were the world's superpowers, and each, predictably, did its imperialistic best to dominate the others. However, in those good old days the reason for national conflict was usually simple greed, the desire to possess territory and to control trade routes. Israel changed that. Rather, I should say, Israelite religion changed it. If "Moses's God *is* God," as Pharaoh Yul Brynner complained in *The Ten Commandments*, then everyone else's god . . . isn't. Over the long haul this basic principle can lead to, certainly lends itself to, intolerance.

Even in biblical times, as Jon Levinson shows,[2] the Israelites deliberately misrepresented the religions of their neighbors. In order to maintain Jewish separateness, scripture doesn't just criticize other beliefs, it caricatures them, making them appear foolish and unattractive. Christianity and Islam in their militant phases — and one has to wonder if either has yet transcended its militancy — still extol their particular versions of monotheism at the expense of others. But what would you? If our particular version of truth is not Truth, then religious faith becomes relative and, ultimately, even Jim Jones is justifiable. If it is Truth, how do we accommodate those who hold otherwise? The dangers of this dilemma are all too apparent.

Jews have been fortunate that only a few times in history have we had the opportunity to exercise power over others; from 135 C.E. to 1948 one looks in vain for significant examples of a Jewish government anywhere in the world. The record of Jewish intolerance toward other Jews, however, is not altogether enviable.

1. S. N. Rosenbaum, "What To Do Until The Messiah Comes: On Jewish Worldiness, *Christian Century* 99:39 (December 8, 1982), p. 1253.

2. J. Levinson, "Yehezkel Kaufmann and Mythology," *Conservative Judaism*, 36:2, Winter, 1982, pp. 36-43.

The celebrated Maccabees forcibly circumcised other Jews, and at about the same time, the Essenes removed to Qumran rather than mix with the impure Jerusalemites.

In the modern period, Jewish Orthodoxy exercises unwarranted power over more liberal denominations in Israel; one reads regularly of Orthodox Jews interrupting Reform services because women are allowed to hold the Torah scrolls. The paradox of modern Israel is that Christians and Muslims have greater religious freedom there than do many Jews. But if some Jews are self-appointed arbiters of the tradition, it is despite a Judaism which, from earliest times, contains a broad streak of toleration.

Even if monotheism is causally connected to modern nationalism, the Jewish version contains safeguards that mitigate the worst excesses of particularism and exclusivism. A key to this attitude is found in TB Sanhedrin 56-60 "The righteous of all nations have a place in the world to come." To obtain salvation one need not be theologically "right," but "righteous." Elsewhere it is written, "Better a righteous Gentile than an unrighteous High Priest." These observations should show that we have no right to be intolerant of others on the basis of their religious beliefs. But Judaism goes further than this.

The basic premise of Israelite law is that human government shall be a government of law not men (people). The often misunderstood Leviticus 24:20 says, in effect, that the punishment fits the crime and takes no cognizance of any differences in the social status or wealth of litigants.[3]

Moreover, there is more to Jewish law than its letter. Leviticus 19:18 says "love your neighbor as yourself," and if there is any doubt about who your neighbor is, Jew or non-Jew, this is resolved by Leviticus 19:33's admonition to remember that Israelites were aliens in Egypt and consequently mistreated. Judaism does differentiate between adherents and nonbelievers by placing a greater burden of performance, the 613 *mitzvot* ("demands") on the former. But it requires of all people that they refrain from murder, theft, and adultery: the Noachide laws.

---

3. Cf. the so-called Code of Hammarabi, 196ff., with differential punishments depending upon the relative status of victim and perpetrator.

If any strangers wish to worship with Jews (Numbers 15:14), they should be accepted. Zechariah (14:9) foresees a time when "the Lord will be One and His Name One." Meanwhile, we must continue to countenance differences even amongst ourselves. The popular saying has it that where there are two Jews there are three opinions. The Talmud itself is just such a record; of its 523 chapters, 517 contain disagreements over what the law should be. It was only later that law became case-hardened.

One of the better known Talmudists was R. Nathan of Gimzo, nicknamed *Gam zu* ("that, too") because when faced with contradictory expositions of particular points, he would say *"Gam zu v'gam zu dibrei 'elohim hayyim."* ("Both this view, and that, too, are the words of the living God.") This ability to rationalize differences and defend various points of view knows no bounds. One of my favorite *midrashim* deals with rabbinic attempts to defend Cain!

The murderer of his brother may be exonerated on at least three grounds. First, they argue, Cain was justifiably upset that God played favorites. Second, Cain accuses God of the crime by giving humans the capacity to get angry ... Third, while admitting the deed, Cain explains that since neither he nor anyone else had ever seen a dead person he expected Abel to get up. Of course, this is fanciful, but it has a serious point: the worst of us are not beyond redemption and, by implication, the best of us are only human. As Job 4:18f, has it, if God finds fault with his angels, how much more so with those who dwell in houses of clay?

Religion is, by definition, that which binds us together. But beyond the boundaries of this or that faith, even of monotheism, lies the horizon of our common humanity. Despite the misapprehension of Matthew 5:43, Jews are not taught to hate their enemies (cf. Aboth de Rabbi Nathan, B. "God will uproot from the world everyone who hates his fellow man."[4]

From the foregoing, it should be apparent how Judaism sees the limits of religious toleration: namely, very broadly. The present paper is far too brief to allow the fuller discussion that the subject demands. Perhaps one final example will show that, despite its

4. Cited in J. Goldin, *The Living Talmud.* New York: NAL, 1957, p. 108.

dangers, monotheism need not lead to a war of all against all. In Deuteronomy 20:19 God gives instructions for beseiging a city:

> When you are beseiging a city for a long time, you shall not destroy its trees by wielding an axe against them .... Are the trees men that they should be besieged by you?

If God takes such concern for trees, how much more so for those who dwell in houses of clay? And since he does do so, we are enjoined to do likewise.

**Preserving the Integrity
of an Institution**

Preserving the Integrity of an Institution

Nearly two decades ago the Tower of the Sun dominated Japan's Expo70 in Osaka where the theme was "Progress and Harmony for Mankind." Visitors to this gigantic tower began their journey deep in the earth in an exhibition entitled simply "Life," passing quickly to the appearance of human life. Prominent in the theme exposition was the realization that humans have nearly always seen themselves as dependent on a presence greater than themselves and that peoples of the world have felt this in many different ways.

Here and there remarkable groups of people developed corporate consciousnesses as they contemplated their shared response to matters of ultimate concern. Jews and Hindus are heirs of such perceptions. From time to time persons of deep spirituality and far-reaching vision appeared, such as Jesus of Nazareth, Muhammad, and Gautama Siddhartha. Their spirituality and their visions became institutions in the years following. Each developed its own hierarchy and its own claims to truth. These became some of the "religions" of the world.

Religion and the religions have become some of the most important creative impulses in the world, and they have proved to be highly successful cultural packages. In so doing they have developed traditional understandings that can serve to check on the validity of individual human experiences. Except in most unusual cases, we no longer explore concerns of ultimate Reality on our own as solitary individuals. Information does not just "float around the universe at random; information to *be* information has to be codified, channeled, protected, and received. Between humans, it can then be shared and transmitted from one life, or from one generation, to another."[1]

Adherents maintain that their information is so important that it must be preserved and transmitted. This requires boundaries — to keep the faithful in and to keep the infidels out. What is being protected is not words only, it is behavior patterns, insights, techniques, social organizations, the regulation of sexuality, and so on; and much of it is transmitted by non-verbal means.

Since the information that is being preserved and transmitted has developed over such a long period of time, there is an understandable reluctance to change. It is not surprising that in times of tension — and our lives are full of it — a strong and assured position will have wide appeal. Religious leaders — popes, imams, sheikhs, pundits, and gurus — remain "boundary-minded."

Centuries rolled on, and near the end of the twentieth century of the present era, we find ourselves in a world where boundaries overlap. American society — the focus of our inquiry — is by nature and definition pluralistic. Despite our motto *e pluribus unum*, our oneness cannot negate our differences. Sometimes we can work in harmony; often we cannot. Just as frequently we minimize our differences so much that we cannot really understand why harmonious cooperation is so difficult.

Few areas of life pose greater problems in human relations than religion, and this volume has collected twenty-one essays, each in its own way addressing the limits of tolerance among persons of many differing religious communities and persuasions. The writers of these papers conferred with each other in a three-day colloquy sponsored by Gettysburg College, Wilson College, and the Pennsylvania Humanities Council in March of 1987. The confrontation was enlightening and helpful, but not easy.

---

1. J. W. Bowker, "The Burning Fuse: The Unacceptable Face of Religion." *Zygon*, 21/4 (December 1986), p. 419.

Twenty participants, nurtured in vastly differing environments, talked freely with each other about the survival of unique spiritualities in a pluralistic setting. They were asked to identify the values of their traditions and those factors they saw as most meaningful and significant in them and then to explore the intricate web of interrelationships with other ways of life and faith, delineating as clearly as possible what it is that inhibits, prevents, or prohibits communication and fellowship.

As the colloquy developed — it was not planned this way — three emphases came to the fore. Some of us trust human experience more than historic institutions or well-defined communities. At the opposite extreme were those whose concern was with the integrity — one might say "purity" — of the institutions to which they had given their loyalty. For others, life in like-minded communities took precedence over either institutional or theological concerns as well as over individual experience.

Because in the popular mind religious commitment is usually identified with institutions, this volume opens with four essays whose authors have deep concern for the institutions with which they are associated. Uma Saini expounds the position of the Hindu Arya Samaja, which she defines as "a society of ... noble people," whose way of life springs from the ancient Vaidika Dharma, which Ms. Saini considers to be the oldest form of Hinduism, expounded in later centuries by Swami Dayananda.

The Unification Church is a much more modern phenomenon, stemming from the teachings and the charisma of the Rev. Sun Myung Moon. It has been in the news frequently, and persons all over the country have strong feelings about this organization and about its founder. Robert Chaumont's treatment of the questions of tolerance and intolerance with respect to this group is important.

Scott Gustafson and Charles Teague write from specifically Christian perspectives. Gustafson moves back to fourth century Christian orthodoxy and its application to contemporary times. Based on the proposition that "Jesus is God incarnate," Gustafson shows clearly the limits of tolerance for anyone maintaining this position.

Charles Teague, on the other hand, objects to the word *tolerance* and then goes on to show a Baptist affirmation on the commonality of all humanity and their ultimate unity in Christ. His essay concludes with a consideration of the "wall of separation between Church and State," but, he points out, it is a wall with windows.

The following divisions of this volume will express quite different points of view.

—H.M.B.

Each person has much in common with
humanity. It is not so much that we need to
seek relationship with one another as to
recognize that which already exists.

3

Freedom of Religion: The Freedom to Draw Circles

Charles Teague

An artist does not paint heroic scenes in pallid hues, nor should a
Baptist present this noble theme through the bland notion of "tolerance." It is deserving of the bolder language of deep conviction.
And so the assigned title is received with marked reservation. To
tolerate something suggests a lingering annoyance, as in one who
tolerates his neighbor's barking dog. A tolerant man would not
poison the dog food, but neither would he grieve should the veteri-
narian put the dog to sleep.

The Baptist position has been stated eloquently and repeatedly.
Writing in the *Virginia Chronicle* (1790), Pastor John Leland expressed it well:

> The liberty I contend for is more than toleration. The very idea
> of toleration is despicable; it supposes that some have a pre-eminence
> above the rest to grant indulgence; whereas, all should be equally
> free, Jews, Turks, Pagans, and Christians.

Pastor George W. Truett echoed that essential distinction in an address from the steps of the U. S. Capitol on May 16, 1920: "Toleration

is matter of expediency; liberty is a matter of principle. Toleration is a grant of man; liberty is a gift of God."

The Baptist Heritage of Liberty

Bred in the fires of oppression and persecution, Baptists quickly made the cause of religious liberty a stirring watchword. It was a Baptist pastor, Thomas Helwys, who published *A Short Declaration on the Mistery of Iniquity* (1612), the first appeal in the English language for complete freedom of conscience in matters of faith. Helwys was imprisoned for the courage of his conviction, but the voice of liberty could not be quieted. Others accepted as an article of faith that which John Smythe declared: "(T)he magistrate is not by virture of his office to meddle with religion, or matters of conscience, to force or compel men to this or that form of religion, or doctrine."

Religious liberty was a much disputed concept, yet the cause proved to be unstoppable. Its expression reached the New World in the words and deeds of Roger Williams, who founded the first Baptist church in America at his Providence Plantation (later to become Rhode Island). In 1644 he published *The Bloudy Tenet of Persecution*, decrying the role of government in the enforcement of religious practice. It is preferable to allow others the freedom of error, argued Williams, than for believers to lose their integrity and thus fail in their Christian mission. "That cannot be a true religion," he declared, "which needs carnal weapons to uphold it . . . . No man shall be required to worship or maintain a worship against his will."

It was with understandable pride that Truett quoted such an authority as John Locke in proclaiming, "The Baptists were the first propounders of absolute liberty, just and true liberty, equal and impartial liberty." Baptists heralded the freedom of conscience as a God-given right of all persons, in what Williams had deemed "soul liberty." Every individual is directly accountable to his Creator, and thus must not be coerced in matters of faith. Belief is a prerogative of being human, as is unbelief. So strong is this conviction among Baptists that even a parent cannot compel a child in the ultimate decision of faith.

The Commonality of Humanity

In focusing upon individual freedom and the prerogative of everyone to decide for himself in matters of faith, Baptists nevertheless recognize that there are strong bonds by which we are related to one another. To emphasize individuality to the exclusion of commonality would lead to a fractionalized existence. Truly, no man is an island.

Humanity is an inclusive grouping. Even when we seek to be apart from one another, we remain a part of one another. No person can ultimately divorce himself from humanity. To realize this has the effect of making one more tolerant of another.

Baptists affirm the commonality of all humanity as declared in Scripture.

— All are created by God. "Rich and poor have this in common: the LORD is the Maker of them all" (Proverbs 22:2). There is a personal Power in the universe to whom we are all accountable.

— All are kindred. "From one man he made every nation of men, that they should inhabit the whole earth" (Acts 17:26). This point is a corollary of the first. We may not be brothers and sisters, but we are surely cousins.

— All are made in God's image. "So God created man in his own image, in the image of God he created him; male and female he created them" (Genesis 1:27). This means that we all have the capacity to communicate with God, are responsible to him as trustees for creation, and have been given creative capacities.

— All sin. "For all have sinned and fall short of the glory of God" (Romans 3:23). Disobedience, not ignorance, is the fundamental problem of all humanity. This sobering reality keeps us humble before God.

— All are guilty. "For whoever keeps the whole law and yet stumbles at just one point is guilty of breaking all of it" (James 2:10). No one is excused.

— All have conscience. " . . . the requirements of the law are written on their hearts, their consciences also bearing witness . . ." (Romans 2:15). Each of us is given the capacity for moral judgment, knowing we have sinned.

— All are loved by God. "For God so loved the world that he gave his one and only Son, that whoever believes in him shall not perish but have eternal life" (John 3:16). Incredibly, in spite of our guilt God still loves us and has provided a way for our salvation.

— All need Jesus. "Salvation is found in no one else, for there is no other name under heaven given to men by which we must be saved" (Acts 4:12). Jesus Christ is the ultimate answer to every human need.

Each person already has much in common with humanity. It is not so much that we need to seek relationship with one another, as to recognize that which already exists.

But a major caveat must be added. This commonality in no way suggests a universalism. Just because our origin and needs are identical does not mean that our destiny is so. One reason Baptists are reluctant to engage in interfaith dialogue is that efforts to reach the lowest common denominator may abrogate the very substance of our faith.

An Intercultural Paradigm

What then is to be our relationship one to the other? By necessity or by choice, individuals associate in groups. In dealing with the issue of tolerance, it is crucial to have a working model to examine such interrelationships. Thus far we have considered the smallest part (the individual) and the greatest whole (humanity). But problems of intolerance are more frequently manifested between groups.

There are four basic groupings of human interrelatedness. The most exclusive and influential of these concentric groups would be the family, those living in one household and joined by the bonds of a common heredity or legal covenant. The most inclusive of the groups would be humanity.

In the history of religious intolerance, the most pervasive problem involves the relationship not in context of family or humanity, but religious communities and the broader society in which they exist. A community is a grouping of people whose fundamental beliefs, values, and allegiance have brought them together in unity of purpose. A community is a voluntary relationship. It may prescribe the behavior of its participating members in such a way as to promote its beliefs, values, and ultimate allegiance. The prescriptive behavior engendered by such common devotion may be deemed "piety." It would include such practices as Christian baptism, the Islamic Hajj, the Jewish Seder, or attendance at Communist Party meetings. (The latter is mentioned to note that a community is not always "religious" in the classic sense of the word.) Each community develops its own standards of piety. It should never coerce such practices, but it may expel one who fails to meet those standards. And the individual should always be free to dissociate himself from a community.

A society is a more inclusive grouping which exists for practical reasons of self-protection and enhancement of the quality of life. It is thus a necessary as opposed to a voluntary relationship. A society may *pro*scribe certain behavior by its citizens in such a way as to protect its very existence. This proscriptive standard may be deemed "morality," and would include laws against stealing, murder, perjury, and so on. A society has no right to *pre*scribe behavior unless the very existence of the society is threatened. If a society recognizes freedom of conscience, it will invariably become pluralistic, that is, having within itself subgroupings of various differing communities.

Communities may appropriately seek to influence the moral parameters of society. In contrast to their Anabaptist kinsmen, Baptists affirm it is proper for Christians thus to participate in the affairs of society. Moreover, Baptists, affirming that the Creator has endowed all persons with a conscience (Romans 2:15), see it as reasonable for all sincere people to influence the moral standards of society. Former Congressman Brooks Hayes (who also served as President of the Southern Baptist Convention) notes that this applies even to those who are not part of an identifiable religious community. "We have no right to assume that the honest humanist is incapable of contributing to the building of a moral order." It must be emphasized, however, that no community may set *pre*scriptive standards for its society even if constituting a plurality or majority. Thus, Baptists have opposed school prayer when it is the society that dictates the form and nature of that prayer.

Each community within the society stands subject to the proscriptive moral standards. Serious conflict occurs when the piety of the community opposes the morality of the society. The community usually suffers because the society, in its powers of protection (police and military), holds the means of complusion. Because convictions of piety and morality are both strongly held, the conflict may have disastrous results. The dissenting community has three ethical options: civil disobedience (seeking to alter the moral standards of society), exile (disassociating itself from society), or conformity (modifying its own pietistic standard).

Baptists see a strong presumption limiting the society in its restrictions upon a community. There may be occasions in which the proscriptive morality of the society will override the prescriptive piety of a community. Examples from American history would include polygamy, snake handling, and refusal of parents to provide medical attention to seriously ill children. Exceptions such as these should be rare and undertaken only where there is a compelling public morality.

Conclusion

Rather than expressing the issue in terms of "community" and "society," Baptists have more commonly referred to the issue of "Church and State." Summarized by Baptist theologian E. Y. Mullins as the "Religio-Civic Axiom," it is declared: "The state has no authority in religious opinions and practices of men, and the church has no right to dictate to the state."

The political guarantee of this ideal in the pluralistic society we know as America is the initial clause of the First Amendment. It was the influence of Baptists such as Isaac Backus and John Leland that contributed to this primary protection of the Bill of Rights. It was enacted, according to Thomas Jefferson in his response to the concerns of the Danbury Baptist Association of Connecticut (1802), as "a wall of separation between Church and State." It is, I may add, a wall with windows.

In no other land and at no other time in history is this God-given freedom of religion more assured. Baptists are determined to keep it that way, not only for themselves, but for everyone.

SUMMARY OF DISTINCTIONS
BETWEEN COMMUNITY AND SOCIETY

	Community	**Society**
Historic Terminology	"Church"	"State"
Nature	Usually Religious	Civic/Secular
Participation	Voluntary	Necessary
Function	*Pre*scribes conduct in order to promote its beliefs and values	*Pro*scribes conduct in order to protect its very existence
Role Over Its Own	Piety	Morality
Power Over Individuals	Unlimited Persuasion	Limited Compulsion
Concern	Purpose of Life	Protection and Quality of Life
Relation to the Other Group	Smaller than the Society, but not subservient to it	Impartial toward its various and diverse communities

Grace is not a principle. It is an
event in which a person is treated
both lovingly and in a way that is not
in continuity with the person's past.

4

The Scandal of Particularity and the Universality of Grace

Scott W. Gustafson

Any understanding of religious toleration depends upon what is thought fundamental to religion.[1] If religion is understood as a system of truth claims and other propositions concerning reality, religious toleration is somewhat problematic because the propositions in question have salvific implications. Since not believing a certain proposition might undermine a person's salvation, the "live and let live" attitude often associated with certain understandings of religious toleration might better be described by those with such an understanding of religion as "live and let die."

Conversely, religion might be understood in such a way that the variety of religious expressions are assumed to be diverse expressions

1. The following two caricatures of religion are stereotypes, and should in no way be understood as the only two definitions of religion possible. They do, however, represent a caricature of "conservative" and "liberal" Protestantism respectfully. I have obviously excluded any Catholic, Islamic, Jewish, Hindu conceptions of religion. This has been done because the perspective from which I have been assigned to write develops against the background of Protestantism rather than Catholicism, Judaism, or Taoism.

of a more ultimate reality. In this case religious toleration seems logically to follow. However, the toleration of any particular expression that claims ultimate status for itself is quite problematic because such claims undermine the assumption that individual religious expressions are indicative of some other, more fundamental reality. For example, according to fourth century Christian orthodoxy, Jesus does not point to a reality more fundamental than himself.[2] Jesus is God incarnate. If this particular religious expression is abandoned in favor of "a more fundamental truth," then God is other than Jesus, and fourth century orthodoxy is false. Since the truth of orthodoxy depends upon the fundamental status of this particular person, Jesus, any understanding of religion that assumes the penultimate character of particular religious expressions cannot tolerate fourth century orthodoxy without doing substantial damage to orthodoxy's fundamental claim.

In agreement with fourth century orthodoxy, this essay will try to maintain the fundamental status of Jesus in its discussion of religious toleration. This means that neither understanding of religion sketched above can be accepted. The first must be rejected because it asserts the primacy of propositions, and Jesus is a person. Since a person is fundamental, any proposition that seeks to express Jesus will have secondary status because Jesus' presence is always more fundamental than any proposition about him.[3] The centrality of Jesus also prevents the adoption of the second understanding of religion because of the claim that Jesus does not point to some reality more fundamental than himself. This claim has been called the scandal of particularity by those who believe that God's universality prohibits God from being completely revealed in some particular manner. Our astonishment that such an assertion might be

2. Some might argue that Jesus actually does point to a reality more fundamental than himself, namely, the Father. It only need be noted that for the fourth century orthodox, the Father was thought to be equal to the Son and not more fundamental. Indeed, it was the very thought that the Son was less fundamental than the Father against which these people struggled.

3. In a critique of this assertion that Jesus' presence is more fundamental than a proposition about Jesus, the reader should be careful not to assume that Jesus is no longer present. Again, the perspective from which this essay is being written is that Jesus is alive and presents himself in the sacraments, preaching and in "the least of these" (the poor and oppressed). Hence, the sacraments, the poor and preaching are more fundamental than propositions.

made, however, often prohibits us from discovering a reason why God might completely reveal God's self in a particular way. If such a reason is exposed, new light might be shed on the issue of religious toleration particularly for those who maintain Jesus' fundamental status.

The best way to approach this in such a brief essay is boldly to make the claim that God cannot be a gracious God without being fully revealed in some particular way. The meaning of this assertion obviously depends on the meaning of grace. Grace is not a principle. It is an event in which a person is treated both lovingly and in a way that is not in continuity with the person's past. Two points must be stressed. A person who is simply treated in discontinuity with his or her past might not be a recipient of grace. That person could just as well be a recipient of torture; hence, there is a relationship between grace and love. This being said, however, grace is discontinuous with one's past. By all rights, a student should fail a course, but the teacher passes the student for the sake of the student and not the administration. An indigent person repeatedly lies to a pastor in order to get money. The pastor knows that she is being "taken advantage of," but gives money anyway. Everything that the human race has done so far merits death, but God bestows life. All of these are examples of grace. Grace, to use a colloquialism, is "not being treated by the book."[4]

So understood, grace must assume a particular, embodied form. Nowhere is this better illustrated than it is in the writings of Franz Kafka. In Kafka's *The Trial*, the hero, K., is accused of a serious crime. He is not told what the crime is. He is not informed of the location of his trial. He is merely told that if convicted he will face a severe penalty. The rest of the novel depicts K's futile efforts to find some*body* who can either defend him or tell him the nature of his crime. K. realizes that if some*body* is not found he will be treated "by the book" and inevitably punished. *The Castle* is similar. Here a surveyor comes to town. He is told that he has a job to do. He is told that the consequences will be quite serious if he fails to perform his task, but he is not told what his job is. The rest of the book is a

---

4. This is an expression of the biblical idea of grace more than, say, a Neo-Platonic definition which might associate grace with ecstasy.

series of fruitless attempts to find some*body* who can tell the surveyor what to do. He knows that if this particular body is not found, grace will be impossible.

Grace is impossible unless a particular body with the power to dispense with the regulations is encountered. That is to say, grace presupposes the presence of a particular body. In the tradition of Kafka, Joseph Heller says just this in his novel *Catch 22*. Here, the hero Yosarian tries to get out of the military on the basis of insanity. He is told by the camp psychiatrist that this is impossible because regulations say that anyone who asks to be discharged on the basis of insanity cannot be insane because the person in question desires to get out of an insane situation, and that is the sane thing to do. At first the logic of this regulation is quite compelling until Yosarian asks the doctor about a pilot who is quite disturbed. When the doctor tells Yosarian that this man cannot be discharged because another regulation states that a person has to *ask* to be discharged on the basis of insanity, Yosarian understands *Catch 22* for the first time. Yosarian is powerless. If he continues to be treated "by the book," he has no hope. He knows this, so he looks for some*body* with the power to dispense with regulations. He knows that grace is impossible unless such a particular body is found.[5]

Obviously, all this does not prove that grace, as defined, must always take an embodied form. All it shows is that grace is contrary to regulations. The question is, can grace, the contrary of regulations, take the form of regulation. It might if a regulation can encompass all cases, but if this cannot be done, it follows that grace cannot be reduced to a law. Its implementation requires the presence of somebody with power to dispense with laws.

One cannot but see the close parallel between this understanding of bureaucratic regulations and the Pauline understanding of the law. Just as Yosarian did not find military regulations to be a source of grace, so Paul could find no grace in the law. Indeed, Paul was one of the first to observe that if the law is used as a route to salvation, our situation is somewhat Kafkaesque; for, the law tells us what we must do to liberate ourselves from our bondage to death,

5. It is particularly interesting to note that all of the chapters of *Catch 22* are named after people — bodies. This makes more apparent the notion that grace requires a particular body.

and, at the same time informs us that what is required is impossible.[6] If freedom from death is accomplished, somebody else must do it. Like Yosarian and Kafka's "heroes," we too must find a body capable of dispensing with these regulations because they only lead to bondage and death. Fortunately, Jesus is such a body.

Now that the fundamental stature of the particular person Jesus has been assoicated with grace, religious toleration can be addressed once again. In the beginning, it was stated that bestowing ultimate status on a particular religious proposition generally undermines religious toleration because salvation is linked to believing a particular proposition. If, however, the particular expression that claims its own universality is Jesus rather than a proposition, toleration is not undermined. This is so because maintaining the centrality of Jesus is the same as maintaining the fundamental stature of grace. Grace is almost the essence of tolerance because it is an action that disregards regulations, social forces, or concepts that would otherwise exclude another. The life of Jesus expresses this fact again and again. Religious laws said that prostitutes and sinners were not suitable companions, but where do you find Jesus? Social forces prevent association with tax collectors, yet Matthew, the tax collector, is a disciple. Samaritans were thought to be the very embodiment of heresy, but Jesus makes one the example of love. Time and time again Jesus dispenses with regulations and customs that are systematically intolerant. He does so because he embodies grace, and grace dispenses with regulations. Indeed, grace is the presupposition of any convivial encounter between diverse agents. As both God and a mediator of grace, Jesus has the power to overrule anything that might ordinarily undermine one person's community with another and this includes a different religious tradition.

To summarize, this essay has attempted to show that maintaining the fundamental status of Jesus in one's thought promotes rather than hinders religious toleration because holding Jesus as fundamental is the same as maintaining the primacy of grace. Since grace is a presupposition for any conviviality between diverse agents, it appears that maintaining the centrality of Jesus implies

6. Romans 1:18-3:20

toleration if toleration is the same as community of diverse individuals. For the most part this analysis has been more a description of a first principle called Jesus of Nazareth. If it is correct to say that he is both God and the embodiment of grace, the case for religious toleration needs no more justification.

Our view of our fellow man determines
how we will treat him, and our attitude
toward the finality of the "truth" we
feel we have found will determine
how we view others' "truths."

5

How Tolerant Can A Unificationist Be?

Robert Jules Chaumont

In the city where I am presently working, Huntington, West Virginia, there was a somewhat amusing bit of intolerance against us back in 1978. At that time our leader was a young woman, Jamie Sheeran. The Ku Klux Klan, angered by our movement's presence in the town, set out to burn a cross in front of our center. Perhaps reading ability wasn't one of their strong points because the first place they pelted rocks at and burned a cross was the house that was used for meetings of The *Unitarian* Fellowship. A chemistry professor living upstairs, alarmed, called the fire department. When the firemen arrived there was a phone call and an apology: "Gee, we're sorry, we meant to burn the cross in front of the *Unification* Church." There is more.

Several doors down from the Unification Center at that time was the home of a recently married couple, the Mooneys. Yes, that is where the KKK next burned their cross. (The couple moved from the city because of the incident.) The Klan never quite found where our center was, and the two young women who lived there then were spared.

Since I joined the Unification Church in February 1975, I have met with the acts of intolerance hundreds upon hundreds of times. Persecution, ridicule, and misunderstanding are our members' daily food. For a New Yorker like myself, raised on Manhattan Island and as in love with its diversity as was Walt Whitman, meeting all this narrow-mindedness and virulent bigotry has been a constant revelation, and it has led me to many a meditation on the nature of man and society. Yet, before I consider these questions: "Why are we as human beings liable to intolerance?" "How is the Unification Movement promoting tolerance?" "How tolerant can a Unificationist be?" I would like to affirm gratefully how meeting seemingly limitless intolerance has had at least five beneficial effects in my own life.

Benefits of Experiencing Intolerance From Others

Though I am hardly a masochistic person and it does indeed hurt my artistic nature to meet so steadily the slaps in the face the Unificationist daily receives, still, experiencing such continual crucifixion does actually have some quite valuable benefits.

For one thing, persecution has helped me step beyond the secular humanist existentialist outlook I had when I met the church. The hypothesis of a spiritual being, Satan, a basic tenet of the Unification Church, has become distinctly more credible to me over the years. Most members indeed become quite sensitive to the interplay for the invisible spiritual world with the physical visible world around us. This spiritual world has a relatively good Abel-type side and a relatively evil Cain-type side. Seemingly inexplicable human behavior often becomes quite comprehensible as one learns to see how people can be influenced spiritually. Most important, knowing Satan's reality allows us better to counter his challenges to our spiritual health.

Secondly, experiencing constant bigotry allows us to grow in our hearts. By striving to "love our enemy" as Jesus implored us to do, we can come closer to the ideal of true love which our founder Rev. Moon exhorts us in virtually every sermon to achieve. He feels it is our role as religious people to break the cycle of violence and revenge and to be a living sacrifice for others.

Thirdly, persistent persecution helps us develop patience and perseverance. If we can outlast the attacks of Satan, Cain Spirit

World, and intolerant persons — maintaining a loving and compassionate heart throughout — then God, seeing what is happening intervenes to heal us and raise us spiritually. If like Jacob we can persevere in wrestling our angels, eventually they will have to give up and bless us. They will have to repent and change, and persecutors like Saul will become devout men of God like Paul.

Fourthly, being the stepped upon pariah helps us develop a sympathetic connection with all other trampled-upon underdogs past and present. Among our brothers are the Christians in Rome who were thrown to the lions, those seeking religious freedom under totalitarian atheistic communist governments, and the impoverished millions of the Third World.

Fifthly, we learn to appreciate at least in a tiny degree the immense and grievous pain in our heavenly Father's heart. He has seen it all from the beginning — from the misuse of love in the Fall, to the murder of Abel by Cain on down to Verdun, Buchenwald, Hiroshima, and the present deadly geopolitical chess game between America and the Soviet Union. Seeing his broken heart we are moved to want to be true sons and daughters who will help do his Will and create a better world.

Why Are We As Human Beings Liable to Intolerance?

Intolerant actions have been legion throughout history. What provokes us to intolerance? Aside from influences of a negative spiritual world as suggested above, poor physiological states, stress, lack of intellectual vision, impatience, fanaticism, insecurity, fear, arrogance and ethnocentricity may all play their parts on different occasions. Furthermore, our view of our fellow man determines to an extent how we will treat him, and our attitude toward the finality of the "truth" we feel we have found will determine how we view others' "truths."

How Is The Unification Movement Promoting Tolerance?

Unificationism is a mankind-embracing movement; our membership includes persons of every race, nationality and religious background. As we live together in our centers and work together on various projects, we come to appreciate the richness of humanity as a whole. We are each of us becoming "world citizens," overcoming our ethnocentricities and historical enmities, and are learning to work harmoniously to achieve goals for the benefit of the world. In relationship to other faiths, we see ourselves in a younger brother position. Though we feel we have an important "new expression of the Truth" to share (to revitalize and make more complete and scientific what has come before), still we know a humble and respectful attitude toward the older traditions is immensely rewarding. We see God's hand in the formation of all the major faiths. Each religion as well as each Christian denomination has had some particular ministry which can contribute to the wealth of mankind as a whole.

Our founder, the Rev. Sun Myung Moon, has established (among some 500 other world-wide projects) not only an organization called the International Cultural Foundation (ICF) to promote unity of the sciences as well as harmony between science and religion but also the amazing International Religious Foundation (IRF), which sponsors numerous interfaith activities. These activities of IRF include the Youth Seminar on World Religions (YSWR) and the Assembly of World Religions (AWR). The YSWR is for students of many faiths and is an annual pilgrimage to major holy places around the world. The students are accompanied by eminent professors who lecture on different areas of religious history and culture. The purpose of the seminar is to stimulate young people to examine the nature of the religious experience and then to respect, in William James's phrase, the varieties of religious experience. The AWR is a three stage (1985, 1989, 1993) commemoration of the 1893 Parliament of World Religions held in Chicago in conjunction with the first World's Fair. The Assembly is a major congress of world religious believers, seekers, scholars and other pilgrims and it seeks to discover in the spiritual traditions the much-needed resources and inspirations that can help resolve the many crises of our time.

How Tolerant Can a Unificationist Be?

Thomas Jefferson declared, "I have sworn upon the altar of God eternal hostility to every form of tyranny over the mind of man." It is only natural to feel strongly about those things which threaten our most basic values. It is natural to try to resist them. Mankind had to resist destructive forces like the spread of the Third Reich. For a Unificationist, ideologies that negate a religious view of man and promote violent revolution (such as Marxism-Leninism) are intolerable because of the incredible human suffering they have caused (e.g., the millions who perished in Gulag.) We have no desire to live under an atheistic totalitarian system, and we don't wish that fate for our children and grandchildren. We treasure our religious and other freedoms and are willing to fight to preserve them.

The Unification Movement is, in fact, investing tremendous resources at present to stem the spread of Marxism-Leninism and to work for the liberation of the peoples forced to live under it. Peaceful means are the weapons of choice in this battle. Through such papers as *The Washington Times* we are fighting disinformation in the media. We are striving to awaken sleeping Americans through supporting CAUSA USA'S educational programs on the true nature of communism and its historical record of atrocities.

To conclude, as tolerant and as embracing as the Unification Movement seeks to be, there are limits. When confronted with movements that injure people physically and/or spiritually, the Unificationist finds he must put aside toleration and move instead to practice the virtue of courageous action for the benefit of the whole.

Just as Sun and Moon are beneficial to
the world may we be helpful to others.
May we live with learned people in
unity and harmony spreading true love
and friendship in the world. (Ṛgveda)

6

Arya Samaja: The Society That Believes in the Vedas

Uma Saini

Ārya, a Sanskrit word, means a pure, noble, righteous and progressive person. The word *Samāja* means society. The word *Ārya*, does not denote any particular sect or race or country. Therefore, any noble and righteous person — living in India or England or Africa or the Middle East or America or in any part of the world — could be an Ārya. A Hindu, a Muslim, a Christian, a Sikh, a Buddhist or any one can be an Ārya if he or she is practicing a rational way of living. Ārya Samāja is a society of such noble people.

Thus, Ārya Samāja is neither a sect nor a religion. The Ārya Samāja believes in the true form of Vaidika Dharma, that is *Sanātana Dharma* — the eternal Dharma, the original form of "Hinduism," a term given by foreign scholars during the middle ages. The Ārya Samāja stands for the revival of the Vaidika Dharma. "The main aim of the Ārya Samāja is to do good to the world, that is: to promote physical, mental, and social progress" (Principle 6).

India of the seventeenth and eighteenth centuries was divided into many sects and gurudoms. Although almost all the sects accepted the authenticity of the Vedas, they interpreted them to their own advantage. Priests and people were practicing superstitious religious beliefs, rituals, and customs. Hindu society had become very weak through the problems of caste, untouchability, idol worship, child marriage, unavilability of education to women, Sati Prathā, ("widow immolation") and so on. Such were the conditions when Swāmī Dayānanda Saraswatī appeared as a religious, social, and political reformer in the mid-nineteenth century India. He saw Hindus divided socially, religiously, and politically into various cults, creeds, sects, and princely states or kingdoms. Swāmī Dayānanda realized the importance of unity among the Hindus. This unity, he declared, was possible only with the revival of the Vaidika Dharma. In order to maintain the continuity of Vaidika principles and social reforms, the Ārya Samāja was founded by Swāmī Dayānanda Saraswatī, at the request of his followers, on the 10th of April 1875, in Bombay, India.

Ārya Samāja believes in the true form of the Vaidika Dharma, the simple and natural way of life of the original religion based on the Vedas, the most ancient scriptures on earth. The four Vedas are the Ṛg Veda, Yajur Veda, the Sāma Veda, and the Atharva Veda. The message of the Vedas regarding peace, prosperity, happiness, unity, and brotherhood is not only for Indians or Hindus but also for people of all nations and for the welfare of the entire world. In his book *Teaching of the Vedas* Rev. Morris Philip, states, "We have pushed our enquiries as far back in time as the records would permit and have found that the religious and speculative thought of the people was far purer, simpler and more rational at the farthest point we reached in the Vedic age than the nearest and the latest." Professor Heeren has observed in his book *Historical Researches* that the Vedas stand alone in their solitary splendor "standing as a beacon of Divine light for the onward march of humanity." That the Vedas were revealed in the beginning of human creation is the unanimous view of all the sages and seers of India.

The Vedas deal with topics such as God, knowledge, action, devotion, meditation, righteousness, wealth, worldly desires, salvation, renunciation, astronomy, mathematics, medical science, physics, botany, zoology, peace, unity, love, and brotherhood.

Many scholars claim that there is nothing pertaining to human life, material or spiritual, which has not been referred to in the Vedas. Vaidika ideas are in perfect harmony with modern science because they proclaim the slow and gradual formation of the world. Vaidika Dharma believes that there is one Truth (God). One God is called by different names because of the different manifestations, attributes, and powers of God. Brāhma, Viṣṇu, Rudra, and other such names are the various attributes, personifications, and powers of God. For example, as the Creator, God is called Brāhma; as the Preserver, God is called Viṣṇu; and as the Dissolver, God is called Rudra. God is formless and ever-existing.

According to the Vaidika Dharma this world consists of three eternal entities: matter, soul, and God.

— Matter is eternal
— Soul is eternal, conscious and finite.
— God is eternal, conscious, pure bliss and infinite.

Matter coexists with God and with souls. Matter, soul, and God are eternal, that is, they have been existing for all times, and they would continue to exist. Matter, according to the Vedas, when inspired by the activity (*tapas*) of God leads to the entire creation. God brings forth this creation out of and from matter. God does not create out of nothing. God's creation has neither beginning nor end. Creation includes destruction of one phase and the manifestation of another. Souls enter human bodies as well as the bodies of lower animals and creatures. Souls, through these bodies, are able to minimize their weaknesses and bad habits, and maximize their virtues. The human body consists of five sheaths:

— physical sheath which consists of flesh, bone, muscle, five organs of senses, and five organs of action.
— nervous sheath which transmits sensations and feelings.
— psychic sheath which controls mental and emotional activities.
— meta-knowledge sheath and
— meta-bliss sheath.

At the time of death, the soul leaves the first three material sheaths and takes with it the other two sheaths of knowledge and bliss. This knowledge and bliss is passed over from body to body making all humans beings different from each other. Souls are free to act and are responsible for their actions. Their present is decided by their past deeds and their future depends on their present deeds. This is the Vaidika philosophy of rebirth and action (karma). It is believed that only the body perishes after death, not the soul, because it is by nature immortal. The soul follows the cycle of birth after death and death after birth. It is always discarding an old body and entering a new one. One reaps good or bad results according to one's own deeds in the present life and in the life to come. It is said that as you sow so shall you reap. This theory of karma explains the diversity in this world. The Arya Samāja believes in the acceptance of suffering as the philosophy of karma, and that suffering ought to be counteracted with right knowledge. The right knowledge brings enjoyment that the soul enjoys by its direct consciousness. This direct consciousness, this bliss, springs from God. This bliss is called salvation, liberation, or mokṣa, the highest objective of a human life according to the Vaidika philosophy.

In order to attain salvation a human being must increase the potentialities of true knowledge and bliss by inculcating the moral and ethical values. The Vedas classify ethical values as patience, forgiveness, self-control, non-stealing, purity of thought, word and deed, control over desires, discrimination between right and wrong, attainment of knowledge, truthfulness of thought, word and deed, and absence of anger.

The uniqueness of the Vaidika Dharma is that its existence does not depend on the biographies and teachings of one or two prophets or saints as is the case with many other religions. Vaidika Dharma is based on the Vedas (the books of knowledge), given at the time of creation. Professor Max Müller also claimed in his writings that if there is a God who has created heaven and earth, it will be unjust on God's part to deprive millions of souls born before Moses of the divine knowledge.

The Vedas contain prayers for physical, mental, and spiritual peace and prosperity. "May the days be peaceful and nights be peaceful. May God bring wealth, prosperity and mental tranquility to the entire world." "May we be un-afraid of the known or the unknown. May we be fearless during the nights and the days. May we be protected from all directions, and may peace come to us from everywhere" (Yaj. 36:11, Athv. 19, 15, 6).

The spirit of giving, sharing love and brotherhood is seen in the Vaidika prayers. "God bless me with food and prosperity so I can help other people of my society. Make my heart as big as the earth" (Yaj. 3:5). "... I may live promoting true knowledge, friendship and brotherhood in this world" (Ashvalayana Grhyasootra, 1, 10, 12). According to the Vedas all of mankind should live harmoniously together as a family (vasudhaiva kutumbakam). A keen desire for universal love and friendliness is seen in the Vedas: "May I look upon everyone with an affectionate eye. May we look at everyone with a friendly eye" (Yaj. 36:18).

The message of the Vedas and the Vaidika Dharma is the message of peace, happiness, unity, and brotherhood. Vaidika message is not limited to one particular type of people, sect, or nation but it is for all human beings regardless of their nationality, race, and current religious preferences. The Vedas stand for social ethics and dedication to society. One of the best ways of loving God is to love all fellow beings. Dedication to the service of others who are weak and righteous from the tyranny of the strong and vicious is the duty of every human being. The problems confronting today's world are very complex and gigantic. Nations, sects, and dogmas are fighting in the name of God. Even two branches belonging to the same sect are becoming hostile to one another. Religion is being limited to the temples, churches, and mosques. Let's not do that. Let's practice religion. Let our lives be guided by religion, the Vaidika religion, which is reflected in Buddha's message of compassion, Mahavira's message of non-violence, Christ's message of service and Muhammad's message of brotherhood. Let God be the inspiring force. "Just as Sun and Moon are beneficial to the world may we be helpful to others. May we live with learned people in unity and harmony spreading true love and friendship in the world" (Rgveda 5:51; 15).

Defining the Boundaries
of a Community

Defining The Boundaries of a Community

The primary fact of religious life in our time is its plurality. If this were not so, no one would feel haunted by the impulse to discover the limits of religious tolerance. In fact, religious tolerance would be a meaningless expression.

There never was, of course, a time when all religious expression conformed to a single norm. Human communities, whatever their *raison d'etre*, have always impinged on each other, forcing on themselves a sense that "the other" was different — and therefore aberrant, perhaps even a threat to one's own self-understanding. That sense of human diversity is clearly embedded in the myths and other cultural artifacts created by historic communities.

In our time, however, that sense of diversity may be devastating. We may prefer to live in religious isolation, but in fact we can no longer hide from each other. The consequence is an intensified realization of the differences among us. We more easily now threaten and feel threatened by each other. Race, ethos, history, and geography are some of the factors that pluralize human societies and set the stage for conflicts that may be violently acted out or subli-mated in myriad ways. Among all possible factors, the diversity of religion is the one that creates the most subtle responses to the many differences that fragment the human communities of this world.

This cluster of essays from the Colloquy on the Limits of Relig-ious Tolerance exemplifies that subtlety remarkably well. On the one hand, each writer is aware of the distinctive character of his/her religious community. On the other, most are reluctant to define a religious identity that requires the denial of the integrity of others. There is minimal agreement, then, that tolerance is a virtue, even though an ambiguous one. Still, practicing this virtue may strain one's own commitments, unless tolerance is itself required by the logic of those commitments. Or perhaps one may manage a be-grudging acceptance of those who live by a truth that violates one's own habits of mind. Some, however, may be moved to a positive affirmation of differences, indeed to a celebration of the pluralistic diversity that confronts them in "the real world."

But in all of these cases "the limits of tolerance" has no meaning for those who have not first defined the boundaries of their relig-ious community. One of the most dramatic pleas that such defini-tion is important is in the essay by Subananda dās, who insists on the validity of choosing to be a unique people, willing to under-go the rigors of religious "virtuosity." But even for those who do not retreat into a radical enclave of religious practitioners, it is only as persons who participate in a community that any of us will dis-cover how far we can go or should go in practicing this ambiguous virtue of tolerance. Hence, the seven essays are distinguished efforts to define the boundaries of religious community. We should not assume, however, that each writer took that as a self-conscious or explicit task. The assignment was simply to reflect on the limits of religious tolerance from within a nurturing community. These essays, from all of those submitted, fall along a spectrum between the poles of *affirmation* and *assent*. The difference between the "ex-tremes" is subtle but significant.

There are those who "affirm" differences of religious persuasion, exhibiting a positive and restless willingness for dialogue. On this end of the spectrum we find those, secure in their own community, who believe that even "heresy" is safe, since the ultimate truth is still unfolding and even revelation is progressive. At this extreme, we find an impatience that wants all doors open to allow passage in both directions. To affirm others in their particular identities is to warrant the validity of the traditions that help to shape them. One writer is so open to dialogue that he is even cautious of the virtue of tolerance: "We cannot afford to be tolerant, if tolerance allows benign neglect." Plurality, then, beckons some to a positive affirmation of other persons and of the religious traditions that contribute to their identity and their differences.

At the other end of the spectrum are those who are able only to give "assent" to the religious differences in a pluralistic world. Here personal religious identity quite dramatically reflects one's connections with a particular tradition. As John Borelli says, "Persons with a religious past will think and act in ways that appear natural to them but which are identifiable with their traditions." Such an observation cuts both ways, of course. It applies both to those who would be tolerant and to those who are "tolerated."

On this end of the spectrum, assent means acquiescence. When those who patiently observe the great variety of differences in the world outside of a particular community, they may "consent quietly," practicing the virtue of tolerance while still "bound" by a particular tradition. The etymology of "acquiesce" is clear even to the untrained eye. It grows from the root which means "to keep quiet." Those who acquiesce in face of differences hold their counsel, that is, remain quiet, in the presence of those differences. This disposition is secure enough in its own certainty that it does not seek to deny or denigrate others. Still, secure in its own certainty and hence not intimidated by outside claims, this position responds to what is given, but may not seek out differences for positive affirmation.

There are those, then, who operate along the spectrum between affirmation and acquiescence, but, wherever they find themselves on the continuum, we recognize them as fellow human beings. In our religiously plural universe, we must appreciate such an array of responses that are, in fact, possible.

There are, however, those who will neither affirm nor yield assent to differences. How those *on* the spectrum we have been talking about react to those who cannot accommodate such an ambiguous virtue as "tolerance" is a difficult question indeed. Such persons catch us on the horns of a dilemma: How shall we tolerate intolerance? No essayist in the Colloquy addressed that problem directly. And despite the variety of distinct traditions represented by all twenty of the participants, one suspects that this dilemma is not especially urgent. Even though the seven essayists in this section range from Roman Catholic to Vaisnava, from Muslim to Mormon, none of them willfully abandoned the spectrum ranging from affirmation to assent and acquiescence. Hence we set the dilemma of tolerating intolerance outside of the limits of our immediate concern — though we dare not declare it, in the long run, irrelevant to the human enterprise.

We must, however, be clear what this section is about. In a religiously plural world, how do we, as individuals, define the boundaries of our respective communities? That is the question. And the point of that question is another broader question: What are the limits of religious tolerance that such definitions allow us? Among the seven essays that follow, I have discovered different responses to that question. None of the essayists denies the virtue of religious tolerance. They do, however, respond to the presence of others along a spectrum of dispositions ranging from affirmation to assent, from an insistence on the necessity for open dialogue to a friendly acquiescence. With clear self-definition as a consequence of having been nurtured in a particular tradition, each essayist discovers the limits of tolerance without surrendering his or her integrity. Life within a religious community demands and allows such integrity. It may not constrain a person to affirm the ultimate validity of the experience of others. But, in the present instances, it has not forced anyone to devalue the experience of others.

As one essayist put the matter, "Non-acceptance of others is not equivalent to intolerance" (Paul). How far "acceptance" goes, however, depends on how one defines oneself within the boundaries of one's own tradition. Should we, may we, can we impatiently *affirm* the power and validity of what makes another what he or she is? Or will we patiently *assent* to the religious differences that define our pluralistic world, waiting for the time, inside or outside of time, when the ambiguities of being human are at last tolerable?

The essays are arranged roughly as they fall along the spectrum from "affirmation" to "assent." Let no one think, however, that there are any implications about the worth or integrity of individual essays on the basis of my faulty judgments. My own estimate is, however, that the seven essays are skewed in the direction of "affirmation," though the authors themselves may not agree. If any of the pieces were systematically probed for their assumptions and implications, their placement may have varied. But none of the essays carries the belief that it is the last word in defining the boundaries of community. Hence, any inference about the limits of religious tolerance must be incomplete.

The order, from affirmation to assent, could, of course, have been reversed. All writers, however, acknowledge that religious tolerance is a virtue. The ambiguity built into each essay is determined by the perspective of the individual essayist: "Is my priority set by the clarity of my own experience or is my priority set by my curiosity about the experience of others?" No essay in this set exhibits an absolutely pure priority in this regard. I suppose that's the way the world is, given that the primary fact of religious life in our time is its plurality.   —L.J.H.

Christian witness is declared to be a
complex matter that includes meeting
and cooperating with those of differing
viewpoints on religious questions so
that all may walk together in truth.

7

Looking for Community Beyond Roman Catholicism

John Borelli

Religious persons are shaped by their traditions in more ways than they may ever know. How they approach life, frame its essential questions, react to its tragedies, identify its significances, and pursue its obligations seem to be part of their psychic fabric. Religious persons will always be religious, no matter how often they succumb to the temptation to flaunt secular attitudes; moreover, religious persons will always be religious persons in specialized ways. Religious novelists reiterate these facts in their characters who fail to undo their past. Persons with a religious past will think and act in ways that appear natural to them but which are identifiable with their traditions. This is one of the great marvels of life. The mosaic of particularized behaviors and attitudes among religious persons is spiritually magnificent and uplifting; at times it is astonishing — as if it were expected to disappear or, at least, to be not quite so obvious.

This marvel is similar to visiting a shrine for the first time, like the Sistine Chapel, or the Deer Park in Sarnath, or the Western Wall, or the holy city of Mecca. It overwhelms us when we find the holy place just as we imagined — as if pictures in books, or scenes in movies, or television images were to be doubted. But no, there we are at a place as real as our own flesh. Our senses drink it up, and we feel the anticipated emotions. This surprise and wonder can be explained rationally; yet, it gives us pause for wonder.

I was still amazed, as I prepared this essay on the Roman Catholic position in reference to the limits of religious tolerance, at how very much my own position, not as a believer but as a scholar, has been shaped by my religious tradition. For a Roman Catholic to write a essay on religious traditions and the limits of tolerance there exists as excellent a collection of documents as can be found in any particular tradition. Perhaps, this is the characteristic of a Roman Catholic approach to inquiry — check the official statements and assess one's personal position in the light of that documentation.

I am very much a child of the Second Vatican Council and have come to maturity in its aftermath. The official Roman Catholic position is clear enough, especially if one were to consult these documents: "Decree on Ecumenism" (*Unitatis redintegratio*) [1964], "Declaration on the Relations of the Church to Non-Christian Religions" (*Nostra Aetate*) [1965], and "Declaration on Religious Liberty" (*Dignitatis humanae*) [1965]. There are numerous other documents produced by the Vatican secretariats for Christian unity, for non-Christians, and for nonbelievers as well as by the Pontifical Commission for Peace and Justice, all of which develop in some detail the general positions in the named documents. One of special importance is "The Attitude of the Church towards the Followers of other Religions" [1984], which marked the twentieth anniversary of the establishment of the Vatican Secretariat for Non-Christians.

I am also a historian of religions, which means that I approach religious data in a certain way too. I am committed to understanding religious persons not only in their particular historical and cultural contexts but also against the larger backdrop of the whole history of religious persons. Though it has its roots in the last century and did not burst abruptly upon the scholarly scene as the Second Vatican Council exploded within the Catholic tradition, the history of religions method is also a feature of the twentieth century. Today it provides an introduction to religious studies on many campuses and has caused a revolution of attitudes both within and outside the academy on the teaching and study of religious traditions. Like the Darwinian revolution in the biological sciences, the general theory has transformed the way we approach a certain area of knowledge although disagreements and arguments abound within the field regarding certain mechanisms and the adequacy or consistency of particular explanations.

The parallel between the unfolding of the official Roman Catholic position on interreligious relations and the development of the history of religions method is striking. I can list four common features: (1) both were founded on an appreciation for diversity, (2) both have taken shape through an anthropology that incorporates sacred experience, (3) both have expressed a profound commitment to intellectual, as well as "lived," dialogue, and (4) both have steered a middle course between purely descriptive objectives and overly zealous theoretical reductionism. This last point is most important for a discussion on religious traditions and the limits of tolerance.

As a Roman Catholic who is informed on the work of the church in interreligious matters and equally as a historian of religions with more than a dozen years experience of teaching and research, I feel a tension, that is at once creative and challenging, while attempting to justify a methodological position to two audiences. A Roman Catholic who is committed to interreligious work must at times explain to Roman Catholics, as well as to other Christians, why this work is neither simply a facet of social justice work nor a new dressing on missionary labors. A historian of religions who wishes to avoid the intellectual nihilism of the modern world must explain to other scholars why this discipline is neither purely descriptive work nor, on the other hand, an academic veneer disguising a high powered approach to religious education in a particular tradition. I have felt this tension at clergy meetings and multireligious dialogues, at academic conferences and curriculum debates. Let me explain the four common features and then reflect on this tension.

When one reviews the various journals and proceedings of the Second Vatican Council and consults with those who were present at the sessions and participated in the committees, one learns how the Council Fathers discovered quickly the importance of the gathering and thereby gave momentum to a process that churned out many policy statements and documents of extraordinary consequence. What was to be a document committing Roman Catholics to improved ecumenical relations with a final chapter on Jewish relations became, over the course of four sessions, three documents that have transformed the Roman Catholic mission dramatically. From a position that could best be described as a mild tolerance of Protestants, non-Christians, and non-believers, bishops of the Roman Catholic Church acknowledged the importance of freedom of conscience, the rewards of cultural and religious diversity, and the mutual enrichment of dialogue and cooperation. The documents anticipated the next twenty years, for in that time Roman Catholicism has become a third world tradition and has been a major participant in ecumenical and multireligious cooperation. At the last synod in Rome, there was a plurality of bishops from the third world. Today, there are more Catholics in Africa, with its massive population of Muslims and wide dimensions on issues of enculturation, than in the United States. The successful work of bilateral discussions and the far-reaching consequences of multilateral meetings and organization have directed the energies and shaped the hopes of people of good will everywhere. Increasingly religious inquiry, theological discussion, and spiritual reflection occur within an ecumenical and multireligious context.

Without giving up a position on true religion, that is, professing and acting in ways that witness God's self-manifestation in Christ and calling of all persons to communion in the apostolic and Catholic Church, Roman Catholics have stated officially that freedom of conscience must be respected, non-Christian religions are means to truth, and that diversity of practice and expression among Christians should be maintained for the life of the Church. An optimistic anthropology, namely that a person is someone called by God to realize the fullness of human nature in divine communion, has given shape to these ideas. This is commitment to an enterprise, not just to tolerance. It is a mission that recognizes sacred experience surrounding humanity, that esteems the achievements of diverse religious communities, and that leads one to sincere and honest dialogue. Christian witness is declared to be a complex matter that includes meeting and cooperating with those of differing viewpoints on religious questions so that all may walk together in truth. The interpersonal feature of dialogue insures that mutual enrichment will result from patient, honest, and friendly sharing.

Although the Roman Catholic position on religious liberty was forged during the cold war, it echoes well in a world that has witnessed the birth of new religious movements and the appearance of religious republics. Within due limits and provided that the just requirements of public order are not violated, the Roman Catholic Church has declared that all persons should be free to organize themselves into communities, to worship as they see fit, to decide on their internal order and ministerial offices without governmental coercion, and to determine the character of family life and the education of children in freedom from outside demands. The penultimate paragraph of the Vatican Council's *Declaration on Religious Freedom* of 1965 foretold well the developments between then and now:

> It is clear that with the passage of time all nations are coming into a closer unity, men of different cultures and religions are being bound together by closer links, and there is a growing awareness of individual responsibility. Consequently, to establish and strengthen peaceful relations and harmony in the human race, religious freedom must be given effective constitutional protection everywhere and that highest of man's rights and duties — to lead a religious life with freedom in society — must be respected.

Irony abounds in history and keeps us from taking ourselves too seriously. Christianity spread in its infancy throughout a Roman world which was extremely tolerant and eclectic in religious matters; but Christians were soon suspected and persecuted for their failure to participate in the political rites of Roman allegiance and citizenship. The Abrahamic fear of idolatry brought torture, death, and exile to inflexible Christians but, it may be argued, gave them the collective character to conquer the pagan world. Once monotheism was in place and Byzantine power undergirded episcopal authority, then deviations from doctrine were not tolerated. It was then the Arians' and Nestorians' turn to go into hiding.

We cannot overlook the history of Western Christian and Islamic relations, more often characterized by suspicion, hatred, fear and ignorance than by tolerance. Roman Catholics also cannot neglect to mention their counterreformation mentality that produced the dark chapters of inquisition and cultural and educational isolationism. Although the documents do not fail to mention that Roman Catholics have not been ecumenical, have not acted kindly towards Jews, and have behaved in ways that were hardly in keeping with the spirit of the Gospel, the irony remains that this same Roman Catholic institution was willing to admit to the whole world, in spite of its history, that no one should be coerced into believing. Furthermore, its relations since the Second Vatican Council gave insurmountable evidence for a policy that the diversity of religious traditions is good and enriching for all persons.

The tension between holding the view that the Catholic Church is the teacher of truth and that all persons should be free to profess their religious beliefs freely in private and public arises primarily from a commitment to a fundamental anthropology that elevates the human person. The same positive view of humanity can be found in the history of religions field. It begins with the presumption that sacred experience has been and continues to be available to persons everywhere, for without the experience of the sacred there would be no living traditions. Secondly, history of religions represents a commitment to understanding religious persons on their own terms and in their own historical, cultural, and religious contexts. One lets the traditions speak for themselves and in their own terminology. Thirdly, since religious beliefs and practices belong to societies everywhere, one looks for larger patterns that are discernible across cultural boundaries. By examining the larger patterns, for example, rites of initiation, cosmic tree symbolism, the story of a great flood, and by learning their specific features in each instance, one's understanding of human nature expands. History of religions is also a product of the post-enlightenment era. Thus, one proceeds critically and conscientiously while interpreting religious data. Careful attention is given so that the material is not altered to fit an interpretation. Finally, history of religions reaches fruition in dialogue, for the scholar must remain in contact with those who are living the tradition as well as those who study it in detail. Someone who is not a Hindu, for example, can be an expert on the tradition; yet, a scholar of the Hindu tradition is sharpened when he/she engages the tradition personally.

The method which I have outlined formalizes my application of the history of religions method. On the one hand, the result is not purely descriptive because of the anthropology on which it rests. On the other hand, it is not a reworked approach to religious education. When all religious traditions are acknowledged as context for the study of any religious topic, one becomes open to the possibility of being shaped by other religious persons. This may result from a policy of honest dialogue as well as from a cross-cultural approach to religious material. One learns quickly the inadequacy of formulae, such as the politicized expression "Judaeo-Christian;" one confronts the injustice of stereotypes, such as the identification of Arabs as terrorists; one realizes the ineffectiveness of arbitrary distinctions, such as "Eastern and Western;" and one transcends the narrowness of self-definitions in general references to "my religion." Tolerance allows benign neglect; dialogue invites a fundamental change of attitude. Our earth is dying from pollution, our societies are disrupted by wars, famine, and violations of human rights, and our world is threatened by weapons of unimaginable power and their aftermath — nuclear winter. We cannot afford simply to be tolerant.

I place no limits of tolerance on
other religious ideas, beliefs, and
practices, to the extent that they do
not put persons at risk physically or,
in a blatant way, psychologically.

8

Beyond Denominational Integrity

Paul D. Gehris

Bloody Mary, in South Pacific, says, "If you don't have a dream, how you gonna make a dream come true?"

The prophet says people shall have dreams and visions. One of my dreams/visions is that in the Creator's good time all creation will become of a piece — together in interdependence. This is my understanding of the way it is supposed to be and can be. The image of the universal lion and lamb dwelling together in cooperation, not competition, depicts a world truly come of age. Ultimately, all systems of knowledge will converge in harmony: the sciences and the arts — both eastern and western.

To enhance this process of convergence, which is a joint venture of Creator and created, I place no limits of tolerance on other religious ideas, beliefs, and practices, to the extent that they do not put persons at risk physically or, in a blatant way, psychologically. I affirm proclamation and modeling. I react against evangelism by threat or by trauma-inducing descriptions of an orthodoxy aimed at coercing adherence.

I am a member of a main line historic protestant denomination —
The American Baptist Churches — United States of America; this
by conception, birth, upbringing, baptism, license to preach,
ordination to professional ministry, and, in my plan, retirement.
Among the strong points of my denomination are
  — responsibility of each adherent to understand Scripture for
  oneself
  — commitment to ecumenism
  — congregational polity
  — personal piety — decided by the person.
Based on my upbringing, formal education, life experience, and
other nursings of my own spirit. I propose some thoughts for this
colloquy. I do not intend to be bound by them when convinced I
should move beyond them. I do not intend to bind any others by
such thoughts, asking only that they receive a hearing and honest
consideration.

Guides for consideration include Bible, Church, orthodoxy,
heresy, and the Holy Spirit. Here the Holy Spirit is considered in
terms of its work through church bodies, congregations, and other
religious traditions as well as through persons who are similar and
different, both in intelligence and in intuition.

The Bible, as I understand it, is a progressive revelation of God
— the ultimate cosmic power, both transcendent and imminent, as
Creator, Sustainer and Redeemer of Creation. The revelation is
ongoing; the creation is still being created; our understanding
grows as we grow. This Bible is not to be demeaned by a literal interpretation or by interpretation through isolated phrases. It is to
be understood as a record of the work of God, written by men, to
be read and understood by persons. It is to me the single grandest
written clue to the nature and purpose of God.

The Church is an institution based on the action of God in the
lives of Jesus and the apostles. It includes the people of God who
come to God through the Christ. It is also an institution in much
the same way as other institutions in our world. It is a bureaucracy
and hence is concerned about size and power, money, influence,
and image. The Church has made and does make positive contri-
butions to society. Libraries, hospitals, colleges owe much to the

vision of the church. In the United States of America it has been the leadership of the church that helped to stop slavery and child labor, supported the right of labor to organize and to negotiate with owners and managers, spearheaded the civil rights movement, and on and on.

Ongoing revelation may make the institutional church a pass-through phase of the search for truth. Denominations and faith groups may be called upon to die or fossilize as new ways of perceiving come to pass. Should that happen, we should remember the past, be glad for it, and not fear the future in its unknownness and untestedness.

The end of the church is not in sight. In the meanwhile, it will do well to be a keeper and sharer of truth and not an inhibitor or blocker of truth.

Orthodoxy is defined as holding to sound or correct theological doctrines. For the church it is preserved in the great creeds which reflect majority votes of great church Councils, and of historical consensus. The Nicene Creed and the Apostles Creed are examples. They reflect truth as known then and can be affirmed now. Wonderfully, however, we have more insight to bring to those creeds today. I affirm the truth of the creeds, not as final truth, but as a good guide towards finding more truth.

Heresy is defined as religious opinion at variance with orthodox or accepted doctrine. It is what separates persons from orthodoxy. Those whose ideas at the great ecumenical Councils did not win the vote found themselves holding heretical views. There has been a bracing, stimulating strain of heresy through the whole history of the church. Could there be meaning in this long life of contrary ideas? The tenacity of heresy through the centuries leads me to believe that there may be some truth or pointer to truth in heresy. While some would blame this on the devil, I doubt that the devil cares that much about orthodoxy to spend energy on heresy.

The Holy Spirit performs God's ongoing work of revelation and action in our time. The Holy Spirit is the presence that will lead us to truth. By heeding the Spirit, "we will know the truth and the truth will make us free." The Holy Spirit works in many ways, through groups and individuals. These include:

Church bodies. These are national and international denomina-tions. The Holy Spirit uses persons, processes, moments in history (*kairos* points), self-understanding, history and hopes of these church bodies to deliver new truth. Maybe a germ or a full-blown concept will be discovered in the working of a church body as it goes about its mission.

Other religions. Major religions, especially non-occidental ones are great repositories of truth. The West, in our ignorance and arrogance, has done too little to learn of the way God has delivered truth to non-westerners. Since World War II there has been some acceptance of the reality of the rest of the world by us, especially including religious and cultural values, up to then dismissed or neglected. Probably the greatest enhancement to our lives will come not from better understanding the nuances of differences between Christian denominations and Judaism, but in learning about and appreciating the basic tenets of the major religions of the East.

Congregations. For the believer the congregation should be home. It should be the place where one can, intellectually, if not physically, "scratch where it itches." The congregation shares many of the gifts of the spirit — apostles, prophets, evangelists, preachers, teachers — to build up the faithful as well as being a setting for the fruits of the spirit — love, joy, patience, kindness, goodness, faith-fulness, peace, gentleness, and self-control. The congregation, or at least those of the congregation who are serious about seeking truth, is the place to ask questions, expand horizons, find different and new meaning in Biblical material and life's experiences. Within the congregation these can be mutual stimulation and support. There need not be agreement, but openness to one another. In the com-munal setting undergirding each other's search is critical for a con-gregation's own health and renewal.

Other persons. Sometimes the helpful other persons are mem-bers of the same congregation. Wherever we find other persons who can be supportive in the search for truth we can use them and be thankful for them. These persons include the following cate-gories:

(1) like mind by like faith. These are persons much like ourselves who could easily be mate or lover, family member or congregational member. They basically share our foundation and values and support the quest for truth.

(2) different mind by like faith. These persons share our foundation and values but are at a different place in the faith journey. No matter. Each person's faith journey must be undertaken personally. It can and should be supported by those of like faith but who are at a different place in their own faith journey.

(3) like mind by different faith or no faith. These persons are near to where we are but come out of a quite different background. These persons can be exciting because they show clearly that we have no corner on truth.

(4) different mind by different or no faith. The only thing in common with persons like these is that they are also on a quest for truth. There is little in common by background or current place in the faith journey. The Holy Spirit proves again a binding of humanity which can boggle the mind especially when we believe we have become unboggled again.

Intelligence. Not only a mysterious "quotient," this is the use of the mind in allowing it not only to dwell on what we know and ponder about truth but also to poke into areas about which we need to learn. Intelligence helps to synthesize new learnings with the old. Intelligence wisely used can lead us to wisdom. Wisdom and common sense can help us to discern the truth.

Intuition. This is a part of my makeup which I early learned not to use, let alone trust. It was not cerebral and not related to intelligence, facts, data, or science. Truly it can be a cheap way to seek truth. But, coupled with intelligence and wisdom, and braced with common sense, intuition can well be a leading of the Holy Spirit into new understanding and truth.

For me, there are no limits to religious tolerance apart from the caveats noted at the outset of this monograph. I believe we must be as open to Spirit of God and the truth of the universe as was Abram, who felt the stirring that there was more than he knew. He is the prototype of the searcher for the truth of faith. Each is called to be an Abram in one's own life, time and way. I believe the Spirit of God calls for that embarkation on journey and supports the journey as the way to discover more of the truth of the universe.

> The "wow" of religious insight, of appreciation, of realization must come to us not of ourselves, but through the other.

9

On the Art of Belonging

Anthony Ugolnik

Years ago, as a young soldier who was trained as an army medic in the Vietnam years, I brought a visitor to a sleepy Greek Orthodox Church in southern Texas, near my army base at Fort Sam Houston. The visitor was a fellow medic. We were best friends, as only the hapless could be. We faced together the ambiguities of that terrible war, which the country had thrust squarely on our shoulders. We had sat through reels of gory training films in that Texas heat, projecting blood and gore which, bad as it was, would never match what we were soon to encounter in the flesh.

Yet close as we were, we were different. In the style of the sixties, my friend was what we used to call a "Jesus freak." Certainly not one of us staidly conservative Eastern Orthodox Christians, he was rapt in the newness of religious discovery. He saw religious experience in individual rather than communal terms. Yet there was something in the ancient harmony of our liturgy which drew him. And when the priest, in those flourishes of Hellenic rhetoric which still survive in our Greek churches, claimed that "some call us a church of the dead — and they are right; we are indeed a church in which the dead and the living intermesh in the inexorable harmony of continuity, of faith, of a living tradition," my friend leaned over to me. In the rhetoric of the sixties, he said a single word in response: "Wow." It was the equivalent of an "Amen" and an "Alleluia," blended together in a single word.

In that inarticulate, yet expressive phrase, at that moment in time, two perspectives met. My friend was remote from us, yet in that very remoteness came the spontaneity, the beauty, of a genuine encounter. In his "wow," I saw much of what I had taken for granted in a new way. And he saw some of his own religious wonder and joy expressed in a way he had never imagined. That friend and I were one — we had met, somehow, in faith. Then, in the late sixties, he was the essence of life and vitality. And now, I teach students born in the year they flew him back to the States in a body bag. In the continuity of a faith, of a living tradition, I still meet that friend and feel my love for him whenever I enter the "Wow," the "Amen" and "Alleluia" of my very specific, very boldly uncompromising Orthodox identity. We became one not sepcifically through *tolerance,"* a word which suggests among us rather too much passivity. We became one through a kind of bold encounter, born of our very differences.

I am a member of a tradition which, in the midst of an age absorbed in its own modernity, focuses upon ancient origins. In a culture marked by its pluralism, Orthodox Christianity is among the most uncompromising in its insistence upon its own status as "the one true Church." We can sometimes be a spur, a prick in the side of polite exchanges which demand a kind of equivalency of respect — a readiness to acknowledge that one perspective is as good, as true, as worthy as any other, so long as it is honestly confessed. We value continuity highly, and we see in our connection through succeeding generations to a line, a procession of faith through the ages, a mark of our validity. Our conception of history interprets the entire human race as a story, living through the ages, drawing all of humanity into divine life through the agency of the Spirit living in the Church. We see the Church as pure. We see it as one. We see it as holy. If tolerance demands that we regard other interpretations as equal in validity, then in this limited sense we cannot be said to be tolerant.

Yet there must be a process, a phenomenon, that can explain the mystery of mutual perfectability — the process whereby my comrade and I, back in the turmoil of Vietnam and the sixties, brought each other closer to God by recognizing what was good and true and beautiful in God and, hence, in each other. That process belongs to no single era or to any single culture, however "pluralistic" or homogeneous its nature. In uncovering that process we discover something transcending tolerance. It is something which lies at the very core of tradition itself.

Eastern Orthodoxy, however uncompromising its position seems to be in terms of western thought, is not narrowly defined on its own ground. Its concept of identity is not based upon the conviction of "subjective rightness," a private ideological self-sufficiency. Orthodoxy conceives of itself as a community, a people confirmed in faith. Its emphasis upon the past is not rooted in a desire to prove its validity as springing from a given era, a primitive era within which the Church and humanity itself came closest to the source of incorruptability. The validity lies in community itself, the link which connects the Church through all ages. Each given age manifests the Spirit, just as does each given culture. No temporal or cultural manifestation is of itself normative. Orthodoxy is the incorruptible community of faith.

The question then arises, how does that community manifest itself? Through every age and in every culture, there is a process of tension whereby identity is confirmed and revealed through dialogue. In Orthodoxy, there is an unrelenting emphasis upon the trinity of God — even God is, in God's very being, dialogic. "God alone is not God," claim our theologians. God utters a word, and the word tends toward a hearer. The trinity of God allows God, by God's very being, to express love.

In the ancient eastern fathers, fast upon the Hellenic age, the roots of a dialogic consciousness stir up controversy as to the nature of God's being. This is important in a dynamic sense, for clues as to the nature of God's being express themselves in our own nature. We are drawn into this divine "inner dialogue," for this trinity creates a momentum, a vortex of love into which we are drawn. Basil, in the early centuries of Christian thought, sees us humans, when we engage each other harmonically in love, as subject to the harmony of the Spirit. Our love for each other, the link between the "me" and the "not me," is a testimony to the life of God in us. We must apply this insight to the question of tolerance. No religious insight could claim absolute self-love as its goal. Love and harmony prompt us to reach out toward "other." Similarly, we as a tradition must not rest in some bizarre conviction of our own self sufficiency. Simeon the new theologian, one of the Orthodox masters of prayer, sees the promptings of love and outreach within us as themselves the consciousness of the Spirit of God, expressing its awareness through us.

In speaking of love, we sometimes speak as if love somehow "belongs" to us. It is possible in English to speak, for example, of "my" love for someone. Love, however, belongs by its nature not only to the one who loves, but to the one who is loved in return. Love and dialogic engagement change and transform — we know what a profound effect our parents have upon our own being, for example. We recognize marriage as a fundamental component of identity. By the end of the Byzantine era, Orthodox theologians like Joseph Byrennois were seeing love as a very constituent of "selfhood." To be human is not to be "self-contained," but rather to engage and be altered by the other. Byrennios sees humans as themselves "reciprocally defined," engaging and altering the other.

This perspective has marked Eastern Orthodox thought into the twentieth century. Thus if we take the elements of Orthodox thought on their own terms, and do not interpret them according to the more individual, subjective terms of the West, we can gain a new insight into the way in which those who seek to love and follow God can engage each other.

First, we must be very careful to acknowledge the frailty of "the word" in human speech. Though God is realized among us, God chooses the fragile, ever-changing dynamic of human interaction to do so. Mikhail Bakhtin, the modern Russian literary critic who was also an Orthodox believer, focuses upon the dialogic process in his work. The word, by which I express myself as an Orthodox believer, exists in a tensile relationship to another. My words tend toward a hearer, and in response the hearer effects a change to sculpt and hew my understanding anew. Each of us is the hand which shapes the other. A review of classic dialogues, like Justin Martyr's exchanges with Philo the Jew, show how in the process of a dialogue two parties effect a change upon each other.

Secondly, once we recognize the charged, ever-malleable dynamic of human speech, we can recognize the source of the dogma and doctrines we cherish. First of all, those doctrines were born in the heat and dialogue of controversy. Our Christian understandings of Christ — as messiah, son of god, prophet and king — are born in the paradigms of ancient Christian communities each of which saw him differently. Thus the dogmas themselves emerge from the tension of dialogue. What is more, those dogmas emerge in the understanding of each generation and each culture as they encounter them.

And finally, and most importantly, we must respect the continuity of identity and religious tradition. For there to be the phenomenon of love, there must be at least the two poles of lover and beloved. For there to be dialogue, which is the very process God has chosen to reveal himself among us from one generation to the next, there must in fact be the separate parties who engage in it. The Nicene Creed, by which I utter and "make real" my own faith in confession, could never have emerged without the dialogic controversies which perfected it. Thus I owe the articulation of my faith not only to those who codified it in that creed, but also to those who in preceding generations engaged the issues it contained, debated them, and brought each other more fully into a consciousness of the faith.

Distinct identity, then, is not something which must be threatened by tolerance. If tolerance should ever alter or challenge the process by which religious believers encounter each other as distinct, even sharply different entities, with different understandings of God, we would undermine the very process by which God "comes to be" among us. It is within this one, true, Apostolic faith, at one with the faith of those who precede me in the Holy Orthodox Tradition, that I can truly and sincerely engage the other. This pluralistic society in which we now live must not be seen as a challenge to any orthodoxy, or as a threat to my own Eastern Orthodoxy. It is rather a fuller opportunity for this divine energy of dialogue and encounter to bring us more fully into engagement. It is only as "myself" that I may truly love others and come to be reciprocally defined by them. Similarly, it is only as an "Orthodox Christian" that I can engage and love those outside my tradition, and come to affect them and in return be affected by them.

My own tradition, in this hemisphere, is only now waking up to its full potential in a pluralist environment. Many among us still feel threatened by pluralism, especially now that all the governmental supports and buttresses of the ancient "Orthodox world," in Russia, in Ethiopia, in Asia Minor, and the Middle East, have fallen into utter and absolute ruin. The Orthodox world is dead, but the Orthodox worldview is not.

In engagement with others, in the years since I left that liturgy in the Greek parish in San Antonio, I have felt its essential mystery. Many times I too, seeing the oneness of God in the eyes of a Jewish or Muslim friend, or the fiber of faith in a Lutheran colleague, or the bonds of sudden communion with a Catholic, felt the stirring of that "Amen" and "Alleluia" the spell of that "Wow" whispered to me by a long dead fellow medic. The "wow" of religious insight, of appreciation, of realization must come to us not of ourselves, but through the other. Some part of my own ancient Orthodox legacy I owe to a friend, a Jesus freak whose name is etched on a wall in Washington, D.C. We owe that which we are to others. This is the plan of God's revelation.

Better to be locked in a cage filled
with fire than associate with those
lacking devotion to God.

10
Religious Virtuosity

Steven J. Gelberg (Subhananda dās)

Since discussions on the challenges of religious pluralism and the
need for interreligious tolerance often seriously question the validity of religious sectarianism — at least in its more absolutist and
insular forms — I would like to offer a friendly apologetic for religious virtuosity (Max Weber's term) and the communalism and social
insularity it often feels it needs to survive. I write not as a detached
observer, but as a long-time member of what might be called a com-
munalistic, other worldly, sectarian religious society, the Krishna
Consciousness movement, a revitalization movement within the
traditional Caitanya (Gaudiya) Vaiṣṇavism of India.

I do not expect to offer, in this brief essay, any conceptual break-
throughs in the analysis of religious sectarianism. My more modest
task, rather, is to make communal religious separateness a little
more comprehensible and perhaps a little less threatening to those
for whom religious faith has not drawn them out of conventional
society, and for whom retreat into what I will call "intensive religious enclaves" may appear excessive, pathological, or antisocial. In
this, my attempt is to extend at least slightly the limits of tolerance
for adherents of such sectarian religious collectives by those who

subscribe to denominations more inclined to affirm the world and the status-quo. As it is the tradition I know best, and as it is my assigned task to speak as an adherent of a particular religious tradition, I will draw descriptive and illustrative materials primarily from the Krishna Consciousness tradition.

In every generation, the world is blessed — or cursed, depending on one's point of view — with a certain number of individuals for whom the world presents itself not as an arena of pleasure, progress, and promise, but as "a slaughter-house . . . one enormous hell," to borrow the words of Nobel Laureate Isaac Bashevis Singer. Many of those who beat a hasty and sometimes desperate retreat from "the world" are those who, as Colin Wilson said, see "too deep and too much."[1] For these sorts of people, the world — with all its infinite vanities, pettinesses, cruelties, deceits, hypocrisies, violence, self-aggrandizement, boredoms, and boorishness — is simply too much to take. Some of them might be able to compromise and adapt, but refuse to; others couldn't if they tried. A refuge, an asylum, is desperately sought. Once sanctuary is found, once a religious haven is established, one creates a religious ideology that includes radical social criticism that both systematizes anti-worldly sentiment and provides justification for having abandoned the world, with all its demands and responsibilities. "Essential religious ideas are so radical," writes psychologist of religion Walter H. Clark, "that only a person who in some sense is a social deviate can follow them. . . . That which deeply criticizes life, as true religion does, must to some degree stand apart from it."[2] Such social apostasy, or world-leaving, is often viewed as more threatening than mere divergence from religious orthodoxy, because it disputes not merely the truth or falsity of this or that theological doctrine, but the very meaning and value of life-in-the-world itself — the life lived in quite good conscience by the wide variety of this-worldly religionists. The conventional Christian, for example, will probably feel less antagonized by the Hare Krishna (Vaiṣṇava) teaching that God is a divine blue cowherd than by its ascetic teaching that a life spent in

1. Wilson has borrowed the phrase, which he repeats periodically in his book *The Outsider* (Boston: Houghton Mifflin, 1956), from the protagonist in Henri Barbusse's novel *L'Enfer*.

2. *The Psychology of Religion* (New York: Macmillan, 1958), pp. 345, 415.

the pursuit of wealth, position, and possessions is a life worthless and wasted. For many, this heresy against the social order is intolerable, and groups that commit it provide a difficult test for the tolerance of conventional, "respectable" religionists.

This social apostasy or retreat from mainstream society, is impelled in large part by a pessimistic view of the material world — a view which is articulated in many of the world's religious scriptures. The *Bhagavad-gītā*, for example, preaches that life in the material world is essentially a condition of suffering. The world as we know it is temporary and full of miseries (8.15), most fundamentally, the sufferings of repeated birth, old age, disease, and death (12.9). The *Bhagāvata-Purāṇa (Srimad-Bhagāvatam)* (5.14.25) classifies the myriad types of suffering experienced in the world as those arising from the innate frailties and imperfections of the body and mind (*adhyātmika*), miseries inflicted upon us by society and by other living beings (*adhibhautika*), and miseries resulting from natural disturbances, such as floods, droughts, famines, earthquakes, and epidemics (*adhidaivika*). The wise person is one who, through diligent spiritual discipline and the gaining of wisdom, seeks a permanent solution to this manifold suffering by extricating from its causes.

When viewing the world in such a manner, the pursuit of comfort, security, success, dominance, fame, and gratification appear not only futile but ludicrous. Perceptions such as these have practical consequences for those who hold them. They bring into being what Max Weber calls "world-rejecting asceticism":

> Concentration upon the actual pursuit of salvation may entail a
> formal withdrawal from the "world": from social and psychological
> ties with the family, from the possession of worldly goods, and
> from political, economic, artistic, and erotic activities — in short,
> from all creaturely interests. One with such an attitude may regard
> participation in these affairs as an acceptance of the world, leading
> to alienation from god.[3]

If, as social scientists say, it is personal crisis that precipitates the turning from the world and the conversion and commitment to intensive religious enclaves, that personal crisis may be the natural

3. *The Sociology of Religion* (Boston: Beacon Press: 1964), p. 166.

outcome of experiencing the world "too deeply and too much." Not all who experience suffering, however, leave the world. Those pull out who, by predisposition, are inclined to interpret their suffering within a broad philosophical framework, and subsequently to seek permanent rather than situational relief. Their acute suffering has lead to painful, radical reassessment of self and world, and an enlightened acknowledgement of the world as a brutal and inhospitable place. From this point of view, the resulting distancing from the social world is not a cowardly flight from pain and failure, but a courageous battle with, and heroic transcendence of, the material world and of mass society. Rather than the "flight from the world" characteristic of what Weber calls "the contemplative mystic," the Krishna devotee's stance is more like what Weber calls "rejection of the world": [H]is opposition to the world is psychologically felt not as a flight, but as a repeated victory over new temptations which he is bound to combat actively, time and again."[4] As with other "world-rejecting" sects, ISKCON members "see themselves as instruments of a protest against society on behalf of transcendence."[5]

This rejection is an abandonment not merely of the world in the abstract, but of worldly-minded persons, whose interests are other than spiritual perfection and salvation. In critiquing the state of humanity in the material world, Indian religious and philosophical texts pull few punches. Those who, rather than dedicate their lives to the pursuit of self-knowledge and spiritual enlightenment seek only to satisfy the animal needs of food, sex, sleep, and self-preservation (however these may be dignified and euphemized by an overlay of culture and civility), are identified as *dvi-pada-pasu*, two-legged animals. Materialists are compared more specifically, in one verse of the *Bhagāvata-Purāṇa* (2.3.19) to a variety of animals: (*sva-vid-varahostra-kharaih*): to dogs, because of the obsequiousness with which worldly people must seek employment and sustenance from material masters: to hogs, because such people lack discrimination with regard to eating habits; to camels, because like that animal

---

4. ibid., p. 169.

5. Robert S. Ellwood, *Mysticism and Religion* (Englewood Cliffs, N.J.: Prentice-Hall, 1980), p. 149.

who likes to chew on thorns, they enjoy the falsely pleasurable taste of blood; and to asses, because they are forced to carry heavy burdens with little reward or recompense, either in terms of immediate gratification or in terms of the fulfillment of one's ultimate, spiritual self-interest.[6] Needless to say, the *Bhagāvata-Purāṇa* values truth over tact.

The ascetic author of the *Bhagāvatam* felt that in order to attain liberation from the material world, the sincere spiritual aspirant must remove oneself from the corrupting influence of such illusioned souls (if not physically, then in consciousness). The allure of worldly sense-gratification is so enticing that not only should the ascetic avoid contact with women (the traditional bane of male asceticism), but even with sensually-minded men who are attached to women, and thus have lost their spiritual intelligence, gravity, and austerity (3.31.33-35). "For a person seeking advancement in Kṛṣṇa consciousness," writes Srila Prabhupada, founder of ISK-CON, in his commentary on the *Bhagāvatam* (3.31.34), "such association is more dangerous than suicide."[7] Better to be locked in a cage filled with fire, advises the Vaiṣṇava saint and avatara Sri Caitanya, than associate with those lacking devotion to God, and one should even avoid looking upon the face of those lacking piety.[8] On the other hand, even a moment's association with holy persons is a "priceless treasure" (Bhag. 11.2.30) and "more desirable than life itself."[9] Separation from devotees of Krishna, says Sri Caitanya, is an "unbearable unhappiness."[10]

Such emphatic devaluing of worldly association and equally emphatic praise of fellowship with spiritual persons stimulates and legitimizes the creation of insular communities of like-minded devotees — institutional bulwarks against the world, havens for religious

6. A.C. Bhaktivedanta Swami Prabhupada, *Srimad-Bhagāvatam* (trans. and commentary) (Los Angeles: The Bhaktivedanta Book Trust, 1972), Second Canto, Vol. 1, pp. 161-64.

7. ibid., Third Canto, Vol. 3, p. 386.

8. A.C. Bhaktivedanta Swami Prabhupada, *Sri Caitanya-caritamrta* of Krsnadasa Kaviraja Gosvami (Los Angeles: The Bhaktivedanta Book Trust, 1975), *Madhya-līla* 22.91-92 (*Madhya*, Vol. 8, pp. 378-79).

9. *Brhad-bhagāvatamrta* 5.44. Quoted in A.C. Bhaktivedanta Swami Prabhupada, *Teachings of Lord Caitanya* (Los Angeles: The Bhaktivedanta Book Trust, 1974), p. 341.

10. *Sri Caitanya-caritamrta*, op.cit.: *Madhya-līla* 8.248 (*Madhya*, Vol. 3, p. 246).

virtuosos. In their intentional narrowing of attention, within those communities, to only those things conducive to salvation or enlightenment, insular spiritual fellowships lead their devotees, as Kierkegaard says, "to will one thing." Many in the world tend to view the inhabitants of such collectives as self-absorbed, narrowminded misanthropes. One can, however, view them more sympathetically, as persons for whom finding meaning and truth is of such overwhelming consequence, that they dare not allow themselves to become distracted from the goal by contact with persons possessed of more petty, temporal concerns. Even Jesus may appear somewhat callous when he insists that the serious spiritual seeker ought to leave the spiritually "dead" to meddle in such worldly affairs as the burial of one's own father. Worldly gratifications, however, may distract one from the ultimate goal and thus are "stumbling blocks on the path of self realization" (*Gita* 3.34), as are, by extension, those who promote and practice self-indulgence.

Throughout his commentary on the *Srimad-Bhagāvatam*, Srila Prabhupada describes the purpose and function of such spiritual collectives. Krishna Consciousness centers are meant, most essentially, to be places where persons can detach themselves from materialistic life and absorb themselves in spiritual practice:

> There are many mercantile, scientific and other associations in human society to develop a particular type of education or consciousness, but there is no association which helps one to get free from all material association. For this reason we have begun the International Society for Krsna Consciousness.... by such association [one] will benefit in spiritual advancement ... [and] cut off his attachment to material existence.[11]

Just as in traditional Indian culture an elderly person would renounce his home and family and go to the forest to practice austerities in pursuit of wisdom and liberation, now people of all ages should "take shelter of the Krsna consciousness movement" to live a renounced, spiritual life and thus attain "salvation from this material world."[12] Such intensive spiritual practice in the association of devotees is like "the waves of an incessantly flowing river,"[13] and it lifts one out of the material world into the spiritual world.

11. 3.25.24 (Third Canto, Vol. 4, p. 32).
12. 4.9.67 (Fourth Canto, Vol. 2, p. 82).
13. 4.9.11 (Fourth Canto, Vol. 2, p. 18).

The ashram is a school for the soul, a place to practice detachment from the temporal environment, to gain mastery over one's conditioned nature, one's materialistic impulses.[14] As one retreats from society, the devotee rises above matter through the practice of sense control. This ascetic "suffering" is described by the sociologist Émile Durkheim. A person, he says,

> never rises above himself with more brilliancy than when he subdues his own nature to the point of making it follow a way contrary to the one it would spontaneously take. By this, he distinguishes himself from all other creatures who follow blindly wherever pleasure calls them; by this, he makes a place apart for himself in the world. . . . the suffering which [ascetic practices] impose is not arbitrary and sterile cruelty; it is a necessary school, where men form and temper themselves, and acquire the qualities of disinterestedness and endurance without which there would be no religion.[15]

Though their own scriptures and saints may encourage separation from or renunciation of "the world," this-worldly religionists tend to feel threatened by such extraordinary displays of religious asceticism, fervor, and commitment, especially when the offending pietists criticize the secular co-option of mainline religion. In recent years, some mainline religionists have even forged alliances with secularists and reductionists in their attack upon intensive religious enclaves. With the exception of some evangelical Christians, most religionists who have objected to the presence of "cults" have done so not on theological grounds, but rather on psychological, social, and economic grounds. That is, cults destroy free will, change personalities, break up families, devitalize educational and career aspirations, divest people of wealth and possessions, suppress sexuality, and so on.[16] Religiosity that is privatized, nondemonstrative, and that does not impinge upon the practical and

14. For a more elaborate treatment of life in the Hare Krishna movement, both in theory and practice, see my paper "Exploring an Alternative Reality: Spiritual Life in ISKCON," presented at a conference on "Krishna Consciousness in the West: A Multi-Disciplinary Critique," New Vrindaban Community, July 1985 (to be published in a volume edited by David G. Bromley and Larry D. Shinn).

15. *The Elementary Forms of the Religious Life* (New York: The Free Press, 1965), p. 355.

16. For more on mainline religious response to ISKCON, see John A. Saliba, S.J., "Christian and Jewish Responses to ISKCON: Dialogue or Diatribe?" *ISKCON Review*, Vol. 2 (1986), pp. 76-103.

essential business of getting a degree, a job, and arranging for life insurance, antagonizes no one. It is generally only when parental and societal expectations are disappointed that inquisitorial impulses arise and the deprogrammers are called in. In addition to the writings and actions of many individual Protestants, Catholics, and Jews in opposition to "cults," Christian denominations and Jewish organizations have, acting in official capacity, devoted no small amount of time and effort to denigrate, stigmatize, and actively persecute intensive religious enclaves. [17]

Whether or not such enclaves survive in their present world-renouncing, world-transcending forms, or indeed survive at all, they can bring to mainline religion certain perspectives and offer certain challenges which can, if they are received in the right spirit, stimulate spiritual and ecclesial renewal. What possible contribution to human society can be made by people who have undertaken such a radical rejection of its values and mode of life? "The man rejected by society may be in closest touch with its best interests," explains Walter Clark. "The most essential and effective forms of religious behavior are demonstrated by only a tiny minority, a religious elite." It is this elite, these religious virtuosi, however, who "supply creative energy out of all proportion to their numbers. This influence is the 'leaven in the loaf' of which Jesus spoke."[18] Theologian Harvey Cox writes, "My real fear about new religious movements is not that harassment will drive them out of existence, but rather that it could push them into premature accommodation, and we would lose the critical perspective that religion can bring to a culture in need of renewal."[19]

Though they dissent from the world and from mainline religiosity, and seem often to be at cross-purposes from mainline religion,

17. To provide a few of the more extreme examples: the Missouri Synod Lutheran Church, through its Commission on Organizations, insists that the notion the "cults" brainwash their members is "not mere speculation, but fact," and endorses coercive deprogramming, even of adults, *even when laws are contravened* — in the name of religiously motivated civil disobedience; the Philadelphia and New York Catholic archdiocese distribute among parochial school students cult-bashing "educational" materials drawn exclusively from highly-biased and discredited anti-cult sources; and numerous Jewish organizations routinely disseminate propaganda against stigmatized religious minorities, provide referrals to deprogrammers, and perhaps even subsidize legal activities against them.

18. Walter Houston Clark, op.cit., pp. 415-418.

19. "Playing the Devil's Advocate, as It Were." *The New York Times*, February 16, 1977.

contact and dialogue with intensive religious enclaves could benefit members of mainline religious bodies in a number of ways. Christians, Jews, and others might learn from them, for instance, that the spiritual life deserves our deepest attention and commitment. For most mainline religionists, whose faith is acquired not through conversion but through enculturation and for whom religious life involves little risk and little self-sacrifice, to observe the deep commitment of members of intensive religious communities may motivate them to immerse themselves more deeply in their own faith. Further, in contact with religious "virtuosi," people can be reminded of the rich possibilities for contemplative and ascetical discipline found in their own traditions, and be stimulated to explore more deeply the experiential and transformational dimensions of the religious life. Finally, such contact might stimulate healthy reassessment of uncritically accepted materialistic values, as Professor Cox indicates above, which obscure the immense spiritual possibilities of human life.[20]

Though intensive religious enclaves may offend mainline religionists with strident anti-materialistic rhetoric, theological innovation, non-conforming lifestyles, competition for the unchurched, and even vigorous proselytization of their own sons and daughters, it is the hope of this writer that Christians, Jews, and others, impelled by the same ecumenical spirit that has stimulated increasing interreligious dialogue and cooperation among mainline denominations, will exercise the religious virtues of tolerance, humility, and patience in responding to the presence of intensive religious communities and their adherents, however apparently challenging, irritating, or painful that presence may be. Those who choose not to be tolerant can take solace in the historical irony that society, human nature, and time all conspire to thwart most individual and corporate efforts at world-transcendence.

---

20. For a more elaborate discussion on how dialogue with ISKCON might act as a stimulus for spiritual and ecclesial renewal, see "Christian and Jewish Responses to ISKCON," op.cit., pp. 44-48.

> As they reach beyond their geographical and
> intellectual borders, for internal survival
> Mormons have had to retain an extraordi-
> nary degree of tolerance of other people and
> their life-styles. This kind of tolerance means
> neither accepting nor condoning others' be-
> liefs or actions. Non-acceptance of others is
> not equivalent to intolerance.

11

Nonacceptance is Not Intolerance

Robert Paul

Mormonism's theology compels a believer to genuine tolerance. This is not to say there are no intolerant Mormons; or that the tolerance/intolerance issue is not a dilemma for some. Personality aside, I assess the Mormonism I know and understand. Furthermore, while my own religious perspective obviously shares common ground with other religious traditions, space prevents me from exploring the common treads that bind Mormons to our collective intellectual, historical, and spiritual heritage. Here I briefly explore how the theology and historical tensions and experiences of Mormonism have shaped its mind set and how Mormons (specifically myself) perceive those outside the tradition. In so doing, I will explore the view that within Mormonism tolerance is characterized not so much by moral dilemma as by paradox.

While simultaneously sharing commonalities with the larger culture and a uniqueness within it, Mormon experience represents a microcosm of American religious life.[1] As a distinctly American

---

1. According to historian/religionist (and Non-Mormon) Dr. Jan Shipps and others. See her "Mormonism: The Story of a New Religious Tradition."

religion, Mormonism reflects the American ethos, including the tolerance/intolerance issue. Mormonism was born in controversy, and it matured in a climate of extraordinary tensions. While rejecting primarily a defensive posture, both the Mormon historical experience and its theology, paradoxically, have shaped the capacity for genuine tolerance by those within the sect.

To begin with, Mormonism rejects the claims of historic Christianity: original sin and salvation by grace. This is not to deny that, for Mormons, the essential nature of life is estrangement from — and subsequent reconciliation with — God. Indeed, the essential purpose of life is to come to know Christ as one's personal savior through a process of personal introspection and moral cleansing. And in that process we may be saved by his unconditional grace, not for or in spite of a fundamentally corrupt nature, but because of the balance between divine mercy and justice. Thus, Mormons claim that the essential condition of life is estrangement, they do so with a unique ontological emphasis.

In the Mormon view, man stands in relation to God as the literal and divine spirit-offspring of God. Thus, there is an essential divine goodness about each human soul. The purpose of the mortal probation is for each child of God to find his or her reconciliation with God. Mortality was never conceived to have been an accident, a result of the Fall, but a fulfillment of the divine plan. Thus "Adam fell that men might be, and men are that they might have joy" (II Nephi 2:25). Thus, God's purpose is ultimately eschatological; to wit, "Behold this is my work and my glory to bring to pass the immortality and eternal life of man" (Moses 1:39). A significant corollary of this proposition is that all members of the human family are literally spiritual brothers and sisters.

Since God and man are intertwined in an eternal and necessary relationship, the love of God is direct and real, and it manifests itself in the life of each human soul. God loves each of his children perfectly and completely. We are all God's literal offspring in the divine mystery we call spiritual birth. Hence, I, as a Mormon, have both an obligation and a genuine commitment to love all of God's children — after all, they are my brothers and sisters. I have no choice, nor would I want it otherwise. Therefore, my own personal feelings of tolerance spring directly from a theological understanding of God and the world.

Since God loves all his children infinitely and equally, without condoning particular human actions, and since it is the "work and glory" of God to see us ultimately happy, Mormons believe that all God's children will hear the gospel message, whether in this life or the next. That message will be testified by the pure prompting of the Holy Spirit, the third member of the Godhead. Being divinely created in the spirit, as well as being created physically through the divine process associated with the physical universe, humans have been endowed with "free agency" — the capacity for genuine moral choice. Fundamentally, Mormons are obliged not to convert, but rather to declare. Whether one joins the Mormons faith or not is fundamentally irrelevant; God will provide all his children with the opportunity for divine knowledge. In the words of a favorite Mormon hymn, "God will force no man to heaven." While some may see an implied elitism here, this is not the case. Within Mormon cosmology, genuine happiness is predicated on actions, regardless of temporal or ultimate beliefs.

As a result of these two governing principles — the necessary relationship of man to God, and the infinite love of God for his/her spiritual offspring — I would be neither morally nor spiritually justified in not expressing a genuine tolerance for those of another faith, including those who ostensibly declare no faith. God loves all equally and will in His time provide full enlightenment to those who seek. Thus, there is no moral dilemma embedded in the notion of tolerance. Rather there is paradox: truth and non-truth, acceptance and rejection, belief and non-belief standing side-by-side without self-annihilation.

Perhaps more so than any other major American Christian religion, Mormonism has been a presecuted movement since 1820, when 14-year-old Joseph Smith declared that he had seen and spoken with God. Born in conflict and matured in a hostile culture, Mormonism has had to adapt itself to the demands of a persecuting majority. As a result, many of the attitudes within Mormonism have been shaped by a basically intolerant milieu. Such social dynamics might suggest, even though the Mormon religious ethos has become somewhat conservative, that Mormonism should have become defensive and therefore perhaps self-destructive. To this day, however, the religion has retained much of its original vitality. Thus, as they reach beyond their geographical and intellectual borders, for internal survival Mormons have had to retain an extraordinary degree of tolerance of other people and their life-styles. This kind of tolerance means neither accepting nor condoning others' beliefs or actions. Non-acceptance of others is not equivalent to intolerance.

Finally, Mormons assert that pluralism is not only valued, but is the very stuff of being itself. While a series of revelatory events marked the emergence of Mormonism, those very events also reaffirmed the more basic ontological relationship to one another and to God. We are necessary (vis-á-vis contingent) with God, endowed with divinely created spiritual awareness, exercising genuine free agency (free will). Coercion in any form is quite literally foreign to the very nature of being and existence.

There shall be no compulsion in faith.
—The Holy Qur'ān 2:27

12

There Shall Be No Coercion in Religion

Shaikh Mubarak Ahmad

In the sixth year of the Hejira, Muhammad the Holy Prophet of Islam granted to the monks of the monastery of St. Catherine, near Mount Sinai, and to all Christians a charter which is a monument of enlightened tolerance. By it the Prophet of Islam secured to the Christians important privileges and immunities, and the Muslims were prohibited under severe penalties from violating and abusing what was contained in the document. In the Charter the Prophet himself enjoined his followers to protect the Christians, to guard them from all injuries and to defend their churches and the residences of their priests. (See the appendix for the full text).

This Charter of the Prophet of Islam is one of the greatest examples in human history of the founder of one faith making explicit guarantees honoring the life, liberty, and property of the followers of another faith. Our tolerance of others should emulate that of the prophet of Islam.

If the events across the world were examined it would be found that the root cause of intolerance leading to persecution is often the misunderstanding that emanates from religious bias. It is even possible that religious traditions may be followed to extremes turning intolerance into an integral part of the tradition itself. Therefore, it is not uncommon to notice social and political insensitivity towards other religious cultures.

Today, tolerance is not an issue merely between a person of the Christian faith and a person from the Jewish faith; it is not simply an issue between a person from Islam and a person of the Hindu persuasion. Rather, religion itself is in jeopardy. Religious intolerance is religion's worst enemy.

As a first step in facing this dilemma, we must educate each other in our respective religious traditions marking the limits of tolerance as preached and practiced by the founder of that faith.

Islam Calls: O! Mankind!

God is not merely the first cause. He designs, creates, fashions, guides, and exercises control over the universe at all times. And, to him, shall all be returned.

The Holy Qur'ān, the word of the exalted Allah, revealed to the Holy Prophet Muhammad (infinite peace and blessings of Allah be upon him) opens with the words:

All praise belongs to Allah, Lord of all the worlds, the gracious, the merciful, master of the day of judgement. (1:2-4).

The Qur'ān ends with the prayer:

Say: I seek refuge with the Lord of mankind, the king of mankind, the God of mankind, from the evil of the sneaking whisperer, who whispers into the hearts of men. (114:2-6).

The Qur'ān's usual form of address while exhorting is: "O Mankind," except where commandments, injunctions, and directions are addressed to those who have declared their allegiance. In such instances, the Qur'ān addresses them as: "O ye who believe."

Islam, then, aims at universality. It addresses itself to the whole of mankind as one fellowship. It seeks to save and to join together all mankind into that one fellowship without distinction of region, country, sex, race, color, or language. In Islam there is no discrimination in any of these variables.

However, Islam teaches and insists upon the acceptance and comprehension of the unity of the Creator, which results in the unity and coordination of creation and the unity and equality of man. That teaching is not at all propagated through compulsion.

So far as man is concerned, the notion of compulsion in human life is inconsistent with the divine project of the universe. Islam being in accord with human nature sets forth a teaching, concerning the freedom of conscience and the freedom of belief, which establishes an ideal for the world.

Religious Traditions and Limits of Tolerance in Islam

The Qur'ān clearly states:

> Proclaim: O ye people, now has the truth come to you from your Lord. So whosoever follows the guidance, follows it for the good of his own soul, and whosoever errs, errs only to its loss. I am not appointed a keeper over you. Follow that which is revealed to thee and be steadfast until Allah pronounce his judement. He is the best of judges. (10:109-110).

Types of Religious Traditions in Islam

There are two types of religious traditions in Islam. First, there are traditions with respect to those who have professed their allegiance to Islam. For them, the teachings of the Holy Qur'ān and traditions of the holy founder of Islam (Hadith) apply. Even after having accepted Islam, there is no Qur'ānic penalty in this world for an apostate:

> O ye who believe, whoso from among you turns back from his religion, should know that Allah will soon bring a people whom He will love and who will love Him, a people kindly and humbly inclined towards believers and firm and impervious towards disbelievers. They will strive in the cause of Allah and will not fear the reproach of a fault-finder. That is Allah's grace; He bestows it upon whomsoever He pleases. Allah is bountiful, all-knowing. (5:55).

> Surely, those who disbelieve after they have believed and then go on increasing in disbelief, their repentence shall not be accepted, and they are the ones who have gone astray. (3:73).

Secondly, there are traditions that pertain to those who have not accepted Islam as their faith. Islamic teaching and traditions with respect to both these groups are clear, as amplified below.

> Proclaim: It is the truth from your Lord; wherefore, let him who will, believe, and let him who will disbelieve. (18:30).

There shall be no compulsion in faith. (2:27).

The Limits of Tolerance

Certain limits have been prescribed in the Book of the all-wise Allah. They do not relate to religious tolerance as defined in terms of agreement or disagreement with the faiths of other people. Insofar as the toleration of the beliefs of others is concerned, Islam clearly enjoins freedom of belief. However, the Almighty Allah has specified His limits. These limits are designed to protect and secure the society against undue hazards. These are in the form of specific commandments, injunctions, and directions. Muslims have been advised to keep well within these limits.

Tradition of Freedom of Conscience in Islam

Islam has established an ideal standard in respect to freedom of conscience. God almighty has said in effect: This is the religion of nature which comprises perfect guidance. A perfect Book has been revealed. No other teaching fulfills human needs to a greater degree nor provides greater beneficence for man, nor discloses to man more clearly the ways that bring man nearer to God. It is Islam alone which has thrown open to man all the gates of approach to God. It imposes no compulsion nor does it permit any. In Islam God says: I account compulsion as evil. I proclaim freedom of conscience and guarantee freedom of belief.

The Holy Qur'ān clearly states:

Proclaim, O prophet: This is the truth from your Lord; then let him who will, believe, and let him who will, disbelieve. We have prepared for the wrongdoers a fire which covers them alike. (18: 30)

The purpose of creation would be frustrated if man had not been granted the freedom that distinguishes him from the angels. According to Holy Qur'ān and the practice of the prophet of Islam Hazrat Muhammad Mustafa (eternal peace and blessings of Allah be upon him) everyone is free to affirm his faith voluntarily, or to proclaim his denial without restraint.

Religious Freedom Guaranteed in the Holy Qur'ān

Religious freedom is guaranteed to all human beings in the following verses of the Holy Qur'ān:

And who is more unjust than he who prohibits the name of Allah being glorified in Allah's temples and strives to ruin them? It was not proper for such men to enter them except in fear. For them is disgrace in this world; and their shall be a great punishment in the next. (2:115)

Condemning the extremists and the fanatics, this verse of the Holy Qur'ān constitutes a strong indictment of those who carry their religious differences to such extremes that they do not even refrain from perpetrating outrages against the places of worship belonging to other creeds. They hinder people from worshiping God in their sacred places and go even so far as to destroy their temples. Such acts of violence are denounced here in strong terms and a lesson of tolerance and broadmindedness is inculcated. The Qur'ān recognizes for all men the free and unrestricted right for worship, for a temple or a mosque is a place dedicated to the worship of God and the person who prevents others from worshiping God in it, in fact, contributes to its ruin and desolation.

There is No Compulsion in Religion

There is no compulsion in religion. Surely, the right has become distinct from error; so whosoever refuses to be led by those who transgress, and believes in Allah, has surely grasped a strong handle which knows no breaking. And Allah is all-hearing, all-knowing. (2:2547)

This verse forbids the use of force for converting non-Muslims to Islam. It also gives the reason for prohibiting the use of compulsion: Truth stands out distinct from error. Islam is manifest truth.

Freedom of Worship Guaranteed to Followers of Other Religions

On the freedom of teaching, practice, worship and observance of religion, the following verses of the Holy Qur'ān are extremely instructive:

Surely, we sent down the Torah wherein was guidance and light. By it did the prophets, who were obedient to us, judge for the Jews, as did the godly persons and those learned in the law; for they were required to preserve the book of Allah, and because they were guardians over it. Therefore fear not men but fear me, and barter not my signs for a paltry price. Whoso judges not by that which Allah has sent down, these it is who are the disbelievers. Therein we prescribed for them: A life for a life, an eye for an eye, a nose for a nose, an ear for an ear, a tooth for a tooth, and for other injuries equitable retaliation; and whoso waives the right thereto, it shall be expiation for his sins. Whoso judges not by what Allah has sent down, these it is who are the wrongdoers.

We caused Jesus son of Mary, to follow in their footsteps, fulfilling that which was revealed before him in the Torah, and we gave him the gospel which contained guidance and light, fulfilling that which was revealed before it in the Torah, and a guidance and an admonition for the God-fearing. Let the people of the gospel judge according to what Allah has revealed therein, and whoso judges not by what Allah has revealed, these it is who are the rebellious. (5:45-48)

Guaranteeing Protection to One who Seeks It

And if any one of the idolaters seeks protection of thee, grant him protection so that he may hear the word of Allah; then convey him to his place of security. That is because they are a people who have no knowledge. (9:6)

According to the injunctions of this verse, during wars instigated by idolaters, when an idolater desired to investigate the truth about Islam, he was granted protection, safely conducted to the headquarters to complete his investigation and was safely returned.

Religious Freedom and Tolerance in the Life of the Prophet of Islam

God Almighty divided the life of the prophet into two phases: One phase of hardship and calamities and sufferings, and the other of victory. During the phase of sufferings those high moral qualities might be demonstrated that come into play at such times. During the phase of victory and authority those high moral qualities might be illustrated which cannot be displayed in the absence of authority.

During the period of trials in Mecca which extended over thirteen years, the Holy Prophet demonstrated in practice all the high moral qualities which a perfectly righteous man should exhibit at such a time like trust in God, perfect serenity under sufferings, steady and eager carrying out of duties and fearless courage.

During the second phase, the phase of victory, authority and prosperity, he demonstrated such high qualities as forbearance, forgiveness, benevolence, and courage. He forgave those who had expelled him from Mecca, bestowed great wealth upon those who were in need and having obtained authority over his enemies, he forgave them all.

Facing Total Persecution

In the beginning of Islam the Muslims were commanded that if the enemies of Islam sought, as they in fact did, to wipe out Islam, by force, they would not take up the sword in opposition to them. But then a time came when it was announced in the Holy Qur'ān:

Permission to fight is granted to those against whom war is made, because they have been wronged and Allah indeed has the power to help them. (22:40)

This meant that the wrongdoing of the enemies having reached its extreme limit, the Muslims were permitted, for the safeguarding of the freedom of conscience and freedom of belief, to take up the sword against the sword of the enemy and to continue to wield it till freedom of conscience and freedom of belief were firmly reestablished in human society according to God's design.

Accordingly, the first and foremost purpose of the wars of Islam was, and will always be, to establish the freedom of belief and worship and to fight in defense of country, honor and freedom against an unprovoked attack.

A Historic, Unique, and Unparalleled Example

A Christian deputation from Najran (in Arabia), consisting of sixty persons headed by their chief Abd Al-Masih known as Al-Aqib, came to the Holy Prophet Muhammad of Islam (eternal peace and blessings of Allah be upon him) to discuss the question of what they called "The Divinity of Jesus." The discussion continued at some length. When the question had been fully discussed and the members of the deputation were found to be still insisting on their false doctrine, the Holy Prophet, in obedience to a divine command, invited them as a last resort to join him in a sort of a prayer-contest called *Mubahala*, i.e., invoking the curse of God on the holders of false beliefs. The Christians declined to accept the offer.

The most important event that happened during this discussion in the Holy Prophet's mosque was that the deputation asked permission to depart from the mosque to hold their religious service at some convenient spot. The Holy Prophet said that there was no need for them to go out of the mosque which was itself a place consecrated to the worship of God, and that they could hold their service in it. This was an act of tolerance unparalleled in all the history of religions.

The Teaching and Training of Tolerance by the Holy Qur'ān

In the exercise of religious freedom the principle of tolerance toward the acts of others is governed by the Qur'ānic injunctions mentioned below. Allah, The Exalted, has said:

> Make forebearance thy rule and enjoin equity and turn away from the ignorant (7:200)
> The wronged one who endures with fortitude and forgives indeed achieves a matter of high resolve (42:44)

Toleration Among Members of the Same Faith

Within the domain of religion, freedom depends upon accepting the limits or extremes of religious behavior. Allah exhorts the exercise of moderation in human behavior (7:32 and 25:68) and has set *hudud* or limits which must not be exceeded at all (2:230, 2:188). Having established these limits Allah says:

> Rejoice then, in your bargain that you have made with Him; and that it is which is the supreme triumph. These are the ones who turn to God in repentance, and who worship Him, who praise Him, who bow down to Him, who prostrate themselves in prayer, who enjoin equity and forbid iniquity, and who watch the limits set by Allah. Give thou glad tidings to those who have faith. (9:11-12)

There can be no religious peace or tolerance without first establishing the true unity of God. Because nations, peoples and societies or communities are constituted by different races, religions, colors or creeds, disharmony will continue to be evidenced. We have to practice a true and universal brotherhood attainable only by accepting the true unity of God who created us all. A Muslim has to recite in his prayers forty times a day:

> "All praise belongs to God, the Lord of the universe, Lord of the Christians, Lord of the Hindus, Lord of the Jewish people and others."

Such a practice, while deterring people from acting against each other, also paves the way to the maintenance of mutual accord and tolerance. The concept of the unity of God is not confined to a particular creed or faith but applies to all faiths, colors, creeds, nations, societies, communities, and indeed, to all the universe. The concept of God's unity would have eliminated any idea of regional or limited godheads. In Islam whatever ideas compromise the divine unity are called *shirk* or setting up equals with the Almighty Being. This is the greatest sin.

It is from this point of view that one realizes the great significance of the teaching of the Holy Qur'ān:

Say, we believe in Allah and in that which has been revealed to us, and in that which was revealed to Abraham, and Ishmael, and Isaac and Jacob and the Tribes; and that which was given to Moses and Jesus, and (also) that which was given to the prophets from their Lord; we do not make any distinctions between any of them, and to Him do we submit.

Conclusion

Defending the Freedom of Religion or Protecting the Limits

The important principle taught by the Holy Qur'ān and demonstrated in the life of the Holy Prophet is that it is wrong to imagine that revealed guidance must under no circumstances inculcate resistance to the enemy and should always demonstrate its love and mercy by way of meekness and gentleness. When God observes that his righteous servants are in peril of being destroyed at the hands of worshippers of falsehood and that this would lead to great disorder, He manifests His appropriate design, whether from Heaven or from Earth, for the safeguarding of the righteous and for putting down of disorder; for as He is merciful, He is also wise.

In the end I caution all defenders of religious freedom against crossing the limits that might oppress others in their realms. The Prophet of Islam says: "Let no one oppress another. Beware of the cry of the oppressed, for there is no bar between it and Allah."

Appendix

The Text of the Charter

This is the document which Muhammad, son of Abdullah, God's prophet, warner and bearer of glad tidings, has caused to be written so that there should remain no excuse for those coming after.

I have caused this document to be written for the Christians of the East and West, for those who live near, and for those of the distant lands, for the Christians living at present and for those who will come after, for those Christians who are known to us and for those as well whom we do not know.

Any Muslim violating and abusing what is therein ordered would be regarded as a violator of God's testament and would be the breaker of His promise and would make himself deserving of God's curse, be he a king or a subject.

I promise that any monk, or way-farer, etc., who will seek my help on the mountains, in forests, deserts or habitations, or in places of worship, I will repel his enemies with all my friends and helpers, with all my relatives and with all those who profess to follow me and will defend him, because they are my covenant.

And I will defend the covenanted against the persecution, injury and embarrasment by their enemies in lieu of the poll-tax they have promised to pay. If they prefer themselves to defend their properties and their persons, they will be allowed to do so and will not be put to any inconvenience on that account.

No bishop will be expelled from his bishopric, no monk from his monastery, no priest from his place of worship, and no pilgrim will be detained from his pilgrimage.

None of their churches or other places of worship will be desolated or destroyed or demolished. No material of their churches will be used for building mosques or houses for the Muslims. Any Muslim doing so will be regarded as recalcitrant to God and His prophet.

Monks and bishops will be subject to no tax or indemnity whether they are in forests or on the rivers, or in the east or west, north or south.

I give them my word of honor. They are on my promise and covenant and will enjoy perfect immunity from all sorts of inconveniences.

Every help shall be given them in the repair of their churches. They shall be absolved from wearing arms.

They shall be protected by the Muslims.

Let this document not be disobeyed till the judgment day.

> For most of us it was not the truth claim of
> our traditions that convinced us to join.
> Rather, it was the experience of acceptance,
> purpose, and meaning that got us in.

13

They Took Me In

Anne Myers

My name is Anne Myers. Currently I serve as the pastor of the
Great Conewago Presbyterian Church in Hunterstown, Pennsylvania, where I preach every week that Jesus Christ is "the way, the
truth, and the life" and that no one comes to the Father except
through Him. I am a committed Christian and a committed Presbyterian and am committed to the doctrine of the Reformed tradition.

But, when I reflect on my own life, I recognize that it was not the
truth claim of the Christian Gospel or the doctrine of the Presbyterian Church that brought me where I am. Let me explain.

As a young person of eleven years of age I awoke one hot humid
August Sunday morning to the sounds of my parents shouting at
each other. This was nothing new. My parents fought constantly.
Their fights were brought on by my father's alcoholism and drug
addiction. So, I was accustomed to hearing them argue. But, for
some reason, on that particular morning their shouts were more
than I could take. I thought that if this is all that there is to life, it is
not enough. So, I got out of bed, got dressed, walked out of the
house and into a Southern Baptist Church located a block away from
my house. That was the first time that I had ever been inside a church.

That church met a need in my life, for as soon as I walked in I felt loved and accepted. I soon learned that the source of that love was Jesus Christ. A short time after that I professed Jesus Christ as *my* Lord and Savior and at that time felt a "call" to the ministry.

I went to college with the intention of majoring in languages so that I could serve the Lord as a foreign missionary. There are not many role models for women in the Southern Baptist Church. Women who aspire to leadership positions serve either as Sunday School teachers or as missionaries. I felt that I was called to a service other than teaching Sunday School. Missionary work was my other option.

While in college I took a course in the Hebrew scriptures. It was in that class that I saw in action one of the most remarkable men that I had ever seen in my life, Dr. Bernard Boyd. He emitted love and excitement for the holy scriptures. Yet, he was an academician and scholar. He approached his work with love for the scriptures, and at the same time he was critical in his approach. This was the first time that I had seen such a combination in a person.

Through his influence, I soon changed my major to religion. He encouraged me to go to seminary. I chose to go Princeton Theological Seminary, the seminary from which he had been graduated.

In three years I was graduated from seminary and was ready to work in the parish. While in seminary I had felt a "call" to the local church instead of the foreign mission field. I sent out 75 letters and dossiers to Southern Baptist churches and institutions. Over a period of nine months I diligently sought a "call" in the Southern Baptist tradition. To my surprise, I did not receive so much as one postcard acknowledging that my information had been received. Therefore, I called and invited *myself* to interviews. Nothing came of my diligent search. However, I did receive two job offers from Presbyterian churches. After much prayer and reflection, I decided to leave the Southern Baptist Church and become a Presbyterian.

Again, I became a Presbyterian because I was accepted and appreciated by people in that tradition. I didn't "bail out" of the Southern Baptist church, that church turned its back on me. In other words, I went to a group that appreciated me.

I would venture to say that for most of us it was not the truth claim of our traditions that convinced us to join. Rather, it was the experience of acceptance, purpose, and meaning that got us into the community; it was the community that validated the doctrine, and not the doctrine that validated the community.

Many of us represent different religious traditions. And the fact is that our religious traditions are incompatible with each other because each of our traditions makes a truth claim. And truth claims, by definition, are exclusive.

I am a Christian and I believe that Christianity offers the clearest view of the Truth. Further, I believe that, as a Presbyterian, that Presbyterianism "fine tunes" that picture even more. I recognize, at the same time, that each of you would say the same thing about your belief system.

Thus, I hope that we do not try to look at what each of our traditions has in common — such as belief in God or a love for humanity. Instead, I hope that we listen and appreciate other traditions and see what these traditions have to offer, and recognize that basic human needs are met by these traditions. We will be more tolerant of one another when we recognize that basic human need is being met by our traditions.

Celebrating the
Human Experience

Celebrating the Human Experience

For many, the integrity of institutions or the maintenance of boundaries are peripheral concerns. Existing communities seem unworthy of primary loyalty. Preserving the integrity of such institutions is not possible, their integrity having long been compromised by narrowness, rigidity, and hierarchy. Religious institutions have forfeited much of their vitality, in this view, because they have become preoccupied with their own power and prerogatives. Rather than being applauded for preserving truth, or providing an occasion for community, they are denounced for protecting an enervated faith and for perpetuating outmoded social practices.

Boundaries, too, often seem more hindrance than help. They imply superiority and foster particularity. Naomi Goldenberg, in one of the following essays, sees in them the legacy of tribal allegiances and male bonding. Edward Stolzfus is more accepting of boundaries as a way to guide members in discipleship, but he, too, echoes the call to move beyond boundary-setting. Their approach requires new patterns of inclusion which reflect human connectedness. Characteristics and commitments that divide are downplayed, while commonalities are stressed.

One commonality is our humanity. These essays share a concern for the integrity of other people rather than for the integrity of institutions or boundaries. Goldenberg, for example, promotes "peopleism" for its ability to engender empathy. Our fate is linked with the fate of others, particularly so in a world threatened by nuclear annihilation. This note of interdependence is pervasive in the following essays. Donald Freeman calls for the development of a faith inclusive of all being. This faith will be characterized by sharing and will benefit all participants. Helen Glassman insists that one's life is absolutely dependent on the life offering of each person and creature.

In this view, both institutions and boundaries are artificial and secondary to the experience of faith and human interdependence. The religious task is to overcome the roadblocks institutions place in the way of developing authentic religious experience, to forge connections which transcend existing structures, and to create communities that are less structured and less rigid.

Two commitments underly the promotion of connectedness and the critique of institutions and boundaries: that there is a multiplicity of appropriate perspectives and identities, and that faith is a process, rather than a fixed commitment. The insistence that perspectives and identities are multiple and diverse leads naturally to a distrust of institutions and boundaries because they tend to define single, authoritative norms. These essays call attention to the diversity both within traditions and between one tradition and another. As K. R. Sundararajan notes, acknowledging such diversity within one's tradition undercuts the confidence that answers are clear and definitive, and so is conducive to approaching other traditions with humility. Freeman offers a related idea. Recognizing one's own views as imperfect and still under discussion, he notes, encourages appreciation for the commitments of others. In Glassman's succinct phrase, truth is decentralized. In such a case, it may be found anywhere, and excessive concern for institutions and boundaries impedes the quest.

Anita Ioas Chapman's image of each religious searcher having a mirror to catch the divine light makes the point vividly. Since each receives the same light, the fact that one mirror might go by the name Hindu and another by the name Baptist is of no account. In such a situation, openness is the most appropriate stance. It is not enough to respond with mere acquiescence — the power and authenticity of other traditions must be affirmed.

Goldenberg takes the notion of multiplicity and diversity a step further by applying it to identities. We have many identities, she argues, which we sustain with varying degrees of loyalty. For Goldenberg, to identify herself as a Jew is only a partial description. Other identities — atheist, feminist, human being — must be added to make possible the nurturing of potential connections to others. Institutions and boundary-setters preclude such connections when they define identities narrowly or insist on a primary loyalty.

Closely related to the insistence on multiple perspectives and identities is the second of the underlying assumptions of most of the following essays: that religious faith is the result of a process conducted by individuals, not a fixed commitment defined by an authoritative institution. People create their faith as they act. Truth is not fixed or immutable, it is in process, or becoming. These emphases parallel those of existentialism and Whitehead, and have been prevalent motifs in feminist and liberation theologies. Faith, above all, is a search, not the adherance to an institution, creed, or set of definitions. It is a path, not a resting place.

This understanding shapes many of these essays, although it takes different forms. Chapman uses the traditional image of the path and the less traditional image of the mirror, while Glassman refers to action, commitment, and involvement. Freeman, taking the approach of a social scientist, refers to this as a "faith-development task": a self-conscious effort to be aware of one's faith and to move to another stage.

Conceiving of faith as a process has direct implications for the concept of tolerance. In refusing to regard one's own faith as final and complete, one is obligated to keep constructing one's faith, drawing on the commitments of others for insight, guidance, and support.

This approach casts the debate about tolerance into a different form. Many of the ironies and paradoxes associated with the way religious traditions deal with tolerance stem from their commitment to a truth. These are often truths which the tradition believes to be universally valid. Once the truth is defined, institutions and boundaries are invoked to preserve it. The universal truth which initially animated followers thus becomes a particular truth, and intolerance toward those who fail to recognize the truth is virtually inevitable. Those who celebrate the human spirit avoid this tendency by refusing to rest content with a fixed truth which has been defined and protected by an institution. Truth is dynamic and multiple. In order to safeguard the integrity of one's truths it is not necessary to draw a boundary which keeps the truths of others at bay.

Widespread agreement about the insufficiency of institutions and boundaries, support for the validity of multiple perspectives, and a commitment to faith as a process unite the essays. They part company on only a few issues. The most important involves defining the connections which will unite faith-seekers. In a sense, the disagreements are intrinsic to any approach which relies on a process. The end result cannot be known while the process is still underway — and the process will always be underway.

Still, the essays offer some tantalizing, albeit tentative, explorations. Glassman recommends an openness and radical commitment to life here and now as it happens. Through this response to life, one will be connected to all that exists. For Sundararajan the connection begins with dialogue which approaches others with appreciation, interest, and the recognition of pluralism. Stolzfus admits to some doubts about how completely Mennonites have dealt with such issues. While they have carefully worked out questions of religious tolerance involving separation from the state, they have yet to fully formulate a positive model of tolerance which looks toward working relationships with other, like-minded believers outside their own tradition. Freeman's proposal for toleration and connectedness adopts yet another tack. It concentrates on creating a climate of, in ascending order, acceptance, openness, and complementarity.

Goldenberg works out a definition of connectedness most fully, combining religious, psychological, and political considerations. In her formulation, one would belong to many alternative communities. These would transcend the existing socially-sanctioned communities which are based on the old system of competitive tribal allegiances. On the personal level, the ego would expand as the "I" recognizes that it is present in all other "I's."

Adopting a stance based on the multiplicity of perspectives and identities, the process of faith, and human connectedness predisposes one toward tolerance. Indeed, the essays share a sense that the term tolerance implies an approach more limited and grudging than is appropriate. Compassion, empathy, and generosity of spirit are enjoined, and notions of superiority and exclusivity are discouraged. Relationships with those of other traditions move beyond tolerance toward authentic sharing and interconnectedness.

At least in theory, there are, in this approach, no limits to tolerance. Unlike those whose commitments to institutions and boundaries enmesh them in tensions between particularity and universality, those who celebrate the human spirit tend to dissolve the tension with their conception of truth as a process. Particular truths are not deserving of full commitment, or even of being an equal part of a dialectic. They, and perhaps the religious traditions which nurture them, will be supplanted as broader, more inclusive truths emerge.

It is possible that this means of transcending the particularity-universality dilemma is illusory. To the extent that they accept "provisional" truths or non-constraining traditions and institutions, those who celebrate the human spirit face the same ironies and paradoxes as those more rooted in a specific institution. Some intolerance, ironically, is directed toward the intolerant, those who, in their exclusivity, refuse to move beyond their own institutions or boundaries. There is also a subtle intolerance toward those still rooted securely and unquestioningly in one narrow tradition or toward those resting in an early stage of faith development.

In addition to these undercurrents of intolerance, there is another way in which the stress on multiplicity, process, and connectedness is vulnerable to the same dilemmas as institution-builders and boundary-setters. The strength of the approach, its openness and ability to reach across boundaries, is also, as is often the case, a source of danger. The danger is that this is a faith stance that is more theoretical than actual. It belongs to no tradition, nor is it embodied in any sustaining community.

There is an effort in most of these essays to reject confessional exclusivism without embracing a false universalism. Some imagine a climate of dialogue and authentic sharing among those who will still be rooted in their own tradition. Others suggest forming new, more appropriate communities, and changing the broader society to make it more receptive to such efforts. These various proposals represent a clear contribution to the debate about how to construct alternatives to existing traditions without having to settle for a traditionless, communityless faith.

Although modern in form, the approaches taken by those who reject institutions, existing communities, and fixed truths in favor of celebrating the connectedness of human experience strike a deep chord in the nation's religious history. They partake of Protestantism's impulse to root out obfuscating traditions, pragatism's experiential and experimental ethos, transcendentalism's quest for wholeness and unity, the religious communitarian's interest in shaping new societies, and individualism's concern for autonomy. Even the vision of transcending excessively narrow traditions has its counterpart — the Protestant awakenings and revivals which sought to unite Protestants of all denominations into one evangelical empire. In addition, these essays draw on two of the animating forces of the American experience — the refusal to be bound by the past and the consequent demand to be free to create one's own future.

In the background, too, is the influence of the American experience of religious diversity. Victims of religious persecution have always taken refuge in pluralism. As a Jew, Goldenberg recalls the sadness and anger occasioned by exclusion. Stolzfus, from the Mennonite tradition, carries historical memories of persecution which have been kept alive by the wary relationship between the Mennonites and the government. Those who have suffered under the claim by the dominant tradition that it represents the clearest view of truth are receptive to arguments that uphold the tentativeness of truth claims and the need for openness and dialogue.

In drawing on these rich American resources for their stress on multiplicity, process, and connectedness, these essays carve out a significant place in the debate over religious toleration. Their skepticism about existing institutions and boundaries, and the resulting efforts to find ways of defining faith and faith-communities, celebrate the human experience in ways that suggest what might lie beyond tolerance.

—M. McT.

A Hindu may not be able to speak
meaningfully to one who does not
accept on principle religious diversity
or a kind of universalism which is non-
rejectionist and all-inclusive.

14

Accepting Plurality

K. R. Sundararajan

A religious tradition in relation to other traditions has two kinds of
responses, a certain degree of tolerance and a certain degree of intolerance. In order to enter into a fruitful religious dialogue one has
to be aware of both dimensions of a religious tradition, both the extent of its flexibility as well as the extent of its inflexibility. This is
also important in the context of India, which has been a home for
several religious traditions for a very long time. I intend to explore
the question of the limits of religious tolerance in the Hindu context
from a historical perspective, examining its mode of handling the
problem of religious plurality, with the intention of exposing some
of the theological considerations that are behind its dual responses
of tolerance and intolerance.

India, since the early times, has been the home of several religious
traditions, some of which are indigenous to the Indian soil, and
some which are of non-Indian origin. The Hindu Brahmanical tradition has existed alongside of the Buddhist and the Jaina traditions
since the fifth century B.C. Beside these traditions, there were philosophical schools of the Brahmanical tradition (*āstika*) and schools
which were outside the Brahmanical tradition (*nāstika*), such as

Carvaka, Bauddha and Jaina. Christians and Jews have been on the Indian soil since very early in the Christian Era, and, later, India was also exposed to Islam. The Hindu (Brahmanical) response to the existing religious plurality has been twofold: In regard to the traditions of Indian origin (the *nāstika* traditions), the Brahmanical tradition has been somewhat intolerant, challenging them and refuting their metaphysical and theological formulations. In addition, there was a subtle process of appropriation resulting in some kind of "Hinduization" (or Brahmanization) of these "rebel traditions." In the case of the traditions of non-Indian origin, the Brahmanical tradition has been by and large indifferent to their presence and to their impact on Indian life. The Hindu thinkers, philosophers and theologians alike, have done a great deal of critiquing of the Buddhist, Jaina and Carvaka traditions, interestingly enough, even after some of these traditions have ceased to be influential on the Indian soil. On the other hand we find hardly any evidence from the writings available of their cognizance of the presence of *outside* traditions in India.

In terms of Hinduization of a non-Brahmanical tradition we could cite the example of Gauḍapāda, the grand preceptor of Śaṅkara. Gauḍapāda was actually called a Buddhist in disguise by his opponents within the Brahmanical tradition, especially for his commentary *Māṇḍūkya Upaniṣad*, titled *Māṇḍūkya Kārika*. Generally, many modern Hindu scholars acknowledge the fact that Gauḍapāda was greatly influenced by Buddhist thought in his philosophical endeavors. However, it is interesting to see that for Gauḍapāda himself his formulations were all "Hindu." In *Māṇḍūkya Kārika*, after discussing the concept of levels of reality, an idea which probably led many to accuse him of being a Buddhist in disguise, Gauḍapāda denies explicitly any Buddhist connection by saying, "This was not spoken by the Buddha." As one of the leading historians of Hindu philosophy suggests, for Gauḍapāda, there was no need to acknowledge any influence of Buddhism in his formulations since "the teachings of the Upaniṣads tallied with those of the Buddha." We could thus see Hinduization as a process of appropriation without explicit acknowledgement to minimize the possible appeal and attraction of the *nāstika* tradition for the *āstika* mind.

While Gauḍapāda initiated the process of Hinduization in the area
of Buddhist philosophy, the *purāṇas* and Vaiṣṇava devotionalism
were instrumental in the Hinduization of the Buddha himself. In the
purāṇas, Buddha became one of the manifestations (*avatāra*) of
Viṣṇu, though manifested for the purpose of misleading evil *asuras*
and thus preventing them from gaining spiritual and global
supremacy over others. In the later period, however, the role of the
Buddha came to be seen in a more positive light. For instance, Jaya-
deva in his *Gīta Govinda* states that the purpose of Buddha incar-
nation is to teach humankind how to be compassionate towards
animals. This process of Hinduization could also be noted in the
manner in which early in its history the mainstream Brahmanical
tradition sought to integrate the non-Aryan traditions in India. The
rising importance of Śiva in the Vedic period and the notion of
divine consort in the later devotional schools are examples of the
Brahmanical efforts to accommodate some of the major thrusts of
non-Aryan indigenous spirituality.

This Hinduization process, which has been used by the Brahmanical tradition to deal with the non-Brahmanical traditions, is,
interestingly enough, extended to Christianity, an "outside" religion, in the period of Modern Hinduism. Keshubchandra Sen, a
leader of the Brahmo Samaj, for example, labels Jesus as an Asiatic
and asserts that Christianity was founded and developed by Asiat-
ics, and in Asia.

This is in contrast to the Brahmanical tradition which had simply
ignored the presence of non-Indian traditions in India. This indifference persisted in spite of the fact that the religious fervor of a tradition like Islam occasionally affected the day to day functioning of
the Brahmanical tradition. In South India we are told that a few
Vaiṣṇava temples were destroyed by the early Muslim incursions
into the Tamil country. According to one tradition, Rāmānuja, the
great leader of the Śrī Vaiṣṇava tradition, rebuilt the temple at
Tirunārāyaṇapuram after it was destroyed by Muslim invading
forces. Again it was at the time of Vedānta Deśika (fourteenth century), another leading exponent of Śrī Vaiṣṇava thought, that the
Viṣṇu temple at Śrī Rangam, was raided by the invading Muslim
armies. It is interesting to see that except for one incidental and

indirect reference to the Muslims, the writings of Vedānta Deśika, which are plentiful, take no cognizance of the presence of those outsiders who in some important way affected the religious life of the Vaiṣṇavas of his time! If one reconstructs the religious history of India from the works of the Brahmanical theologians, one would hardly detect the presence of Christians, Muslims, Jews, and Zoroastrians in India. One would, however, gain the impression that the Buddhists, Jains and Carvaka were active theologically even in the fourteenth and fifteenth centuries, when as a matter of fact their influence has declined considerably since the ninth and tenth centuries.

Hinduization is, thus, one of the methods used by the Brahmanical tradition to deal with challenges posed by the non-Brahmanical and outside traditions. In regard to the question what makes the Hindu tradition respond instead of being indifferent to another tradition we can only conjecture. The Hindu tradition responded to Buddhism and Jainism both at the philosophical and popular level. At the popular level, in South India at least, several kings became Jainas and Buddhists and therefore attempts were made to reconvert them. It was the Śaivas, more than the Vaiṣṇavas, who undertook these crusades and succeeded in reconverting some of the kings who had joined the nāstika side. At the philosophical level the challenge of Buddhism was met by Gauḍapāda and Śaṅkara particularly, by a process of rejection of some of its philosophical formulations and also by a process of appropriation thus enriching the Hindu philosophical tradition. In the case of modern Hinduism, Christianity was seen as a serious challenge, especially by the Hindu intellectuals and reformers, who also saw themselves in the role of defenders of faith. This challenge was met by Hinduizing Jesus, and also by projecting Hinduism as the universal religion which has a place in its theological framework for the different religions of the world.

I wonder whether the debates which went on between the Buddhists and Jainas on the one side and the Brahmanical scholars on the other side were not responsible for a hostile response from the Hindu side. It is hard to decide who initiated these debates, but there are stories of frequent public debates. A similar situation existed possibly in the modern times with the denouncing of the Hindu tradition by Christian missionaries, especially in the seventeenth, eighteenth and nineteenth centuries. It is possible that in the case of Islam, since no such serious "debates" took place, excepting at a small scale in the court of the Mogul emperor, Akbar, the Brahmanical tradition simply ignored its presence. A debate, in contrast to a religious dialogue, often tends to focus on the inadequacies of the "opposing traditions" leading to a defensive response from those criticized, instead of stimulating the appreciative interest in other religious traditions as an ideal religious dialogue should.

In regard to religious tolerance, I wish to claim that the Hindu society has generally been permissive and tolerant. The religious tradition has had many critiquing the tradition from within. For instance the Upaniṣads were highly critical of the early Brahmanical ritualistic tradition. However, it is interesting also to see that the Upaniṣads project themselves as continuing the earlier Brahmanical tradition by spiritualizing, in some sense, its ritualistic imagery. On the contrary, the Buddhist and Jaina traditions, as they evolved, saw themselves apart from and discontinuous with, the Brahmanical tradition. The discontinuity was heightened by their rejection of a pattern of life that governed the social structure and religious life of the Hindus. This was one of plurality or diversity which is basic to the Hindu (Brahmanical) social and religious life. The Hindu social structure is hierarchical and also a plural class system (varna) with four major groups. The duties and obligations and even moral codes are different for the members of these four classes. In the area of religious life, the tradition provides a diversity of options in terms of religious disciplines (yogas) appropriate to one's intrinsic nature. In both contexts the notion of svadharma is highly important. While svadharma stands for individual duties and obligations based primarily on one's class (varna) and stage of life (āśrama) (and in an extended sense one's intrinsic nature or disposition), it also underlines the fact of paradharma, the duties and obligations of many others in the society which are different. Svadharma on principle rejects the notion of universal dharma, a universal code of behavior applicable to all classes and to those in different stages of life and to men and women alike. Here we could see the reason for the Brahmanical uneasiness with the Buddhist notion of universal *dharma* and also its hostility to this new critic on the Indian scene. The continuation of the *svadharma* mentality perhaps also accounts for the Hindu "missionary response" to the claims of missionary Christianity.

It is interesting to note that when the modern Hindu thinkers claimed Hinduism to be an universal religion their notion of universal religion was different from that advanced by missionary Christianity in India. The modern Hindu universal religion was based on the *svadharma* model, a model of plurality, where all other religions find a proper place, however, within the framework of Hinduism which provides an overarching unity. This sense of universality was in contrast to the rejectionist, non-inclusive universal model of missionary Christianity. Perhaps Sri Rāmakrishna Paramahamsa was the supreme example of this Hindu universalism, one who has, in the Hindu understanding, been a Muslim, a Christian and an Advaitin, and still prefered to be the devotee of Kali, worshiping her as a Mother, a form of worship close to his heart and therefore in some way natural to him.

The extent or the limit of Hindu tolerance is therefore conditioned by the acceptance or non-acceptance of the principle of plurality by the dialoguing partners. A Hindu may not be able to speak meaningfully to one who does not accept on principle religious diversity or a kind of universalism which is non-rejectionist and all-inclusive. Though the traditional model of diversity included a hierarchical structure (or a staircase notion as some of the modern Hindu scholars would say), it is possible for a contemporary Hindu to dispense with this notion of hierarchy (or sense of superiority) and meet the dialoguing partners on an equal footing for a fruitful culmination of interreligious dialogue.

The need is for us to extend our tolerance to
understand the universality of the human
yearning for truth and to see differing
views as the reflection of that search.

15

Mirrors That Reflect The Light

Anita Ioas Chapman

One of the characteristic signs of this century is that, even as interaction and mutual dependence in international affairs grows, so do
attitudes of bigotry and persecution, particularly in the field of religion. We are increasingly surrounded by people who attempt to
combat change with the weapon of intolerance. Cloaked in the
mantle of religion, walk many with spiritless goals.

My background is that of the Baha'i Faith and the teachings of
Baha'u'llah. The few simple points I will make are based on those
teachings.

Tolerance is an attitude that can be learned: that is, an outward
fact may not change, but one's attitude toward it will change as one
grows, suffers and matures, so that one's perception of that fact becomes broader and deeper. One's own inner development permits
one to appreciate why another holds a certain belief, or practices
his belief in a certain way.

One of the basic Baha'i teachings, one no doubt shared by many
other traditions, is the concept of man's free will. Given his free will,

the beliefs man holds, the practices he adopts, are chosen through the exercise of this God-given freedom. What one does with this power, whether one sleepwalks through life, idly accepts attitudes current in one's environment, or seeks one's philosophy far from one's native shore of belief, is the result of one's own volition. Therefore, though we may not share another's concept, we must respect that he is walking on his chosen pathway.

In several passages, Baha'u'llah refers to God as the Friend. In his mystic work *The Seven Valleys*, he says all people are "wandering in search of the Friend." In Islamic tradition there are many stories of Majnun, the lover, who searches everywhere for Laili, the object of his love, even sifting through the sand for her. When told he cannot find an ethereal creature like Laili in the dust, he replies that he searches for her everywhere, haply he may find her somewhere.

The Baha'i teachings give as the purpose of life this search, and in this valley, says Baha'u'llah, man "rides the steed of patience." Each of us is at a certain point on the path leading to the Ultimate. The need is for us to extend our tolerance to understand the universality of the human yearning for truth and to see differing views as the reflection of that search.

A Baha'i's limit of tolerance has more to do with peoples' unreligious attitudes than with their theology, and he will more likely do battle with attitudes than with theology. For instance, when he sees attitudes at variance with divine law through the ages, he is led vigorously to condemn. A concrete example that may be cited is back-biting, which Baha'u'llah likens to murder. It is the Baha'i feeling that people must be challenged and made to examine their use of this nefarious weapon, which destroys all trust. In other words, a Baha'i finds it difficult to remain silent (tolerant?) faced with attitudes that undermine human society (e.g., racial bigotry), and assumptions that lead to actions that destroy man as a spiritual being.

In the search for reality, definitions are important. To a Baha'i, religion is the "changeless faith of God, eternal in the past, eternal in the future." Each of us is born into a historical religious culture. This is the mirror in which we see the light of divinity reflected, and our mirror is beloved to us through all the associations of our lives with it. It is over these mirrors, then, that we are extending the mantle of our tolerance. It seems useful to make this distinction between the Light and the mirrors, since the object of search is the Light.

There is a need in addressing the question of tolerance, to raise discussions to the level of principle. It is the Baha'i conviction that we need to seek the reality of religion, what its purpose is, why it exists. Do we agree on the singleness of God? Do we agree on the oneness of humanity? Do we agree on the purpose of religion, which in some way is the underlying question posed by the issue of tolerance? Baha'u'llah defines religion as "the outer expression of the divine reality." He also says: "Reality is one, and when found, it will unify mankind."

There are a number of hindrances to a closer relationship among religions:

- attitudes of exclusivity on the part of a religion;
- the need to develop our "distinctive characteristic" (thought) to weigh and analyze belief;
- clinging to theories for which there is no evidence;
- understanding the influence of people, through their interpretations of religious revelation, in creating religious strife.

It might be useful in a discussion of these hindrances to sort out where the hand of man has painted over the hand of God; where the human bricklayer has built over the temple of God with custom, misunderstandings, willful change. Is a particular custom the essence of religion; is it immutable? To answer such questions will be to assist everyone's thinking on the subject. It may be that we belittle religion by thinking of it as this or that custom or ritual.

Baha'is are taught as they grow up to associate in "love and fellowship" with those of other religions. It is therefore difficult for me to deal with tolerance as a concept. I wonder if it does not imply inequality, with us enduring rather than appreciating one another. If love is the essential dynamic of religion, do we not need to move to another level?

There is no wall of separation between
church and state but a moving line and
the amount of toleration is interpreted
in relative, contextual terms based on
society's law and level of acceptance.

16

The Mennonite Experience

Edward Stoltzfus

"And we thank you, our Father in heaven, that we can gather together today in Thy Name without fear of man."

These words of prayer were spoken by the senior minister in most
Sunday morning worship services in the Mennonite congregation
where I grew up. This prayer was burned into my memory and into
the collective consciousness of many Mennonites in North America
until very recent times.

As a boy in the congregation I wondered: What does he mean?
Afraid of what men? And what had we done? Who would want to
terrify us? I could not conceive any possible reason why anyone
would wish to strike fear to that slightly sleepy gathering of God's
children which I saw sitting around me.

That prayer preserved a memory given to us by our European
Anabaptist foreparents of the sixteenth century. They had been
pitched about and pulverized with unrelenting persecution from
church and government authorities, from Catholic and Protestant
leaders. Why? Because the Anabaptist call for an intentional, covenanted community of believers separated from state-church society

arose as a fearsome threat to the unity and cohesiveness of society. The movement could not be tolerated.

Earlier the Roman empire had tolerated a variety of religious opinions and groups. When Christianity was born the ancient Greek gods had already been invited to join the Roman gods in the pantheon at Rome. The gods of the mystery religions were accepted along with the divinities of various pagan tribes absorbed into the empire by military conquest. At first Christianity was considered a part of Judaism and "licensed" under its name. But Judaism was never happy with the arrangement. As Christianity progressively defined itself differently than Judaism, it began getting in trouble with the empire also. It rejected divine honor to the emperor. Finally Trajan declared it illegal around 96 A.D. But it was not destroyed. There alternated times of relative freedom, usually regionally defined. When persecution could not curb its growth, edicts of toleration were issued in 311 and 313 A.D. by the emperor Constantine.

It only took about 100 years, however, for the persecuted Christians to become the persecuting ones. First the emperor Theodosius made Christianity the only tolerated religion in the empire in the 380s and second, the great Augustine provided a theological base for the use of coercion and violence against the Donatists in order to force them into orthodox belief and practice.

From that time on in western Europe until well into the seventeenth century only officially defined orthodoxy (at first Catholic, then Protestant also) united with the state was tolerated. And since there had been a gradual merger of ecclesiastical canon law with civil law as the centuries slipped by, heresy was punishable by death.

Occasionally claims are made that the Reformers in the Protestant reformation are the source of religious toleration. But this is true only in a secondary or tertiary sense. When both Catholics and Protestants discovered they could not militarily force their religious views on the other they grudgingly granted each other a territorial (religious) toleration.

The truth is that Luther, Zwingli, and Calvin completely rejected the notion of religious toleration towards both Catholicism and other forms of Protestantism. Luther declared in 1526: Though it is not our intention to prescribe to anyone what he is to hold or believe, yet we will not tolerate any sect or division in our principality. And Zwingli, the Zurich reformer, made his position clear: Why should the Christian magistrate not destroy statues and abolish the Mass ...? This does not mean he has to cut the priests' throats if it is possible to avoid such cruel action. But if not, we would not hestitate to imitate even the harshest examples.[1]

Calvin's position is well-known. He opposed all forms of religious toleration symbolized by his deep involvement in the burning at the stake of Michael Servetus at Geneva, in October, 1553.

Again we ask: why were all religious persuasions so mutually intolerant? Sidney Mead observes, though, in connection with the American struggle for religious freedom, "Establishment rested upon two basic assumptions: that the existence and well-being of any society depends upon a body of commonly shared religious beliefs ... and that the only guarantee that these necessary beliefs will be sufficiently inculcated is to put the coercive power of the state behind the institution responsible for their definition, articulation and inculcation."[2]

The Anabaptists were the only Reformation group consistently pleading for religious toleration although individuals such as Sebastian Castellio voiced similar calls. In their plea for religious toleration Anabaptism anticipated continued religious pluralism but their cry was stillborn. The emergence of toleration in the west and in America came from other sources.

Nevertheless Anabaptists sounded a clear call:

Conrad Greble, an instigating leader of Anabaptism, in his programmatic letter of 1524 to the peasant leader, Thomas Muntzer, said: "Go forward with the Word ... without command or compulsion, then God will help thee."

1. Walter Klaassen, *Anabaptism: Neither Catholic nor Protestant* (Waterloo, Ont.: Conrad Press, 1973) p. 58.

2. Sidney Mead, *The Lively Experiment: The Shaping of Christianity in America* (New York: Harper & Row, 1963) p. 63. For a sixteenth century defense of religious intolerance see "Urban Rhegius, Justification for the Prosecution of Anabaptists, 1535" in *Sixteenth Century Anabaptism: Defenses, Confessions, Refutations*, tr. by Frank Friesen (Waterloo, Ont.: Institute of Anabaptism and Mennonite Studies, Conrad Grebel College, 1981), pg. 87.

Felix Mantz, an associate of Grebel's and an early martyr, admitted he taught, according to the Zurich court records of 1525 and 1526: "that those of other faiths are to be left undisturbed in their practice."

Hans Denck said: "Everyone should know that in matters of faith everyone should proceed free, voluntary and uncompelled."

Kilian Aurbacher, a Moravian Anabaptist, said to Butzer of Strassbourg in 1534: "It is never right to compel one in matters of faith, whatsoever he may believe, be he Jew or Turk. Even if one does not believe uprightly . . . Christ's people are a free, unforced and uncompelled people."

And Menno Simons, in one of his many comments on this subject, said: "Faith is a gift of God and therefore it cannot be forced on anyone by worldly authorities or by the sword . . . it must be obtained of the Holy Ghost as a gift of grace."[3]

Of course Anabaptists asked for religious toleration so that they could have space to live and breathe and practice their faith, but what did they say was the basis for their request? Bender mentions these four reasons (along with other suggestions): 1) Jesus himself practiced it. He tried to persuade persons into the kingdom of God. He never used coercion. 2) Genuine faith cannot be compelled. 3) Christians are obligated to love everyone, including unbelievers and enemies. This is what Jesus taught and practiced. And 4) Voluntarism in faith is the only valid basis for intentional and accountable church membership.[4] So Anabaptism called for toleration but this toleration was complicated by another part of their theology.

Anabaptism advocated a two-kingdom doctrine. There was a kingdom of Christ and a kingdom of this world. The kingdom of Christ was to be characterized by peace, righteousness, forgiveness, non-violence and suffering love. The kingdom of this world was characterized by strife, vengeance, anger and power by the sword. The church is the visible gathering of those committed to the kingdom of Christ. Governments belong to the kingdom of this world. They are in the ordering of God but outside the "perfection

3. Harold S. Bender, "The Anabaptists and Religious Liberty," *The Mennonite Quarterly Review* (April, 1955): 83ff.

4. Ibid., p. 97-98.

of Christ." They perform a crucial social function whether benevolent or tyrannical. They keep order in society. They are to be respected at all times and obeyed, except when their demands conflict with God's.

Some Anabaptists were more aware of the limitations of this two-kingdom doctrine in terms of sociological realities and some were less aware of the complications, but the fact is that when they perceived two social realities — church and larger society — the meaning of toleration and the limits of toleration needed to be thought through for both. So the limits of toleration is one thing when viewed from the church; it is another thing when viewed from the perspective of the state.

The limits of toleration for membership in the church was spelled out on two fronts, or more appropriately one should say, it was always in the process of being spelled out by the processes of decision-making in the church community: that which was believed and that which was practiced.

Individuals, congregations and larger associations developed confessions of faith composed of dogmatic materials from the church's creedal statements and from their own emerging convictions. The basic commitment was to declare oneself an intentional follower of Jesus, the risen Lord, in accountable relationship with fellow-believers. Various measures were developed within the church community to guide persons in their faith and life. The ultimate sanction was excommunication. It was a sign that a person did not choose to work within the disciplines of a given community of believers. Physical violence or coercion was not employed, only the power of persuasion. But it was precisely at this point that the limits of toleration for group involvement by the individual became an issue. And since Anabaptism emphasized discipleship as the sign of authentic Christianity the "limits" of toleration (for membership) were identified and expressed more frequently on items of the practice of the faith then on items of theological or confessional affirmation. And the test for this was whether a person was living in the character of the love of Christ as seen in the New Testament.

How much religious toleration could a government allow? Anabaptists considered it illegitimate for civil authorities to use coercion in religious matters. For example, Leopold Scharnschlager once made his appeal for toleration to civil authorities on the assumption that people want to serve God voluntarily and without coercion: you [the princes] would not want the emperor to demand of you to give up your faith and accept him. Well, we request that you remember... that this is the situation with me and my associates. I and my kind do not attempt to preserve ourselves and our faith by force or resistance but with patience and suffering, even unto death ... [if you would find it wrong to obey the emperor against your conscience] then I as a poor Christian beseech and exhort you for God's sake and for the sake of your souls' salvation that in this matter you expand your conscience and have mercy on us poor people.[5] And Pilgrim Marpeck insisted that a government exceeded its authority when it sought to surpress or "to root out the false prophets." But Menno Simons, undercutting his many pleas for a religiously neutral government, said that a government was to "chatise and punish... manifest criminals... by reasonable means ... without tyranny and bloodshed...[and] manifest deceivers [meaning many Catholic and Protestant teachers]."[6] Here Menno Simons assumes the common church-state conviction that a society needed well-ordered religious beliefs so that it does not disintegrate into anarchy and these beliefs are to be supervised by the government, with the limitation that it not use violence. But Menno's comment is a minority voice.

So what can we conclude about Anabaptism and its understanding concerning the limits of religious toleration? There are two social-political structures: the church and the state. The limits of toleration are interpreted differently for each. Since the church is made up of voluntary participants it guides the limits of toleration for its own members by internal processes defining faith and practice. The state (of which the members of the church are also participants) defines its limits of toleration on the basis of its political self-interest to have a well-ordered body politic, but, most Anabaptists claimed, it is to be neutral on religious matters. Anabaptism did

5. Leopold Scharnschlager, "Farewell Address to the Strassbourg Council," *The Mennonite Quarterly Review* (July 1968): 214-215.

6. Klaassen, *Anabaptism in Outline*, pp. 296-297.

not explore the limits of toleration except to ask that it include a place for its own minority religious convictions and practices.

Modern Mennonites have been on the edges of debate on tolerable practices based on religious convictions and practices (conscription for military service for example) but they have not self-consciously explored the implications of their residual and somewhat doctrinaire convictions about religious toleration. In their migration to the new world in the eighteenth century they settled gratefully in William Penn's colony with its promise of comparative religious freedom. They could live with Penn's definition of "liberty of conscience" which he had outlined in 1686.

... by liberty of conscience, I mean, a free and open profession and exercise of that duty; especially in worship: but I always premise this conscience to keep within the bounds of morality, and that it is neither frantic or mischievous, but a good subject.... In brief he that acknowledges the civil government under which he lives and that maintains no principle hurtful to his neighbor in his civil property.[7]

Theoretically, Mennonites have considered radical religious pluralism possible in American democratic society yet they know from experience that religious issues are never neutral in a working society. Such matters always impinge on the social and political welfare of others. Therefore in our American context the limits of toleration are continuously being litigated in the courts to gain an interpretation of what can be tolerated and what cannot be tolerated for the general welfare of society. There is no wall of separation between church and state but a moving line and the amount of toleration is interpreted in relative, contextual terms based on law and society's level of acceptance.

There are three levels on which Americans face the issue of the limits of religious toleration: (1) the range for religious belief, (2) the range for speaking or propagandizing religious belief and (3) the range of practice of religious convictions.

7. William Penn, "A Persuasive to Moderation to Church Disserters in Prudence and Conscience," in *A Documentary History of Religion in America*, ed: Edwin S. Gaustad (Grand Rapids, Eerdmans, 1982), p. 119

There is little problem in interpreting the first level: one can have maximum freedom to think and believe as one wills. There is more problem with the second level. How much can the country tolerate the advocacy of antisocial or antigovernment religious practices? For example, can the Mormons advocate polygamy as they did a century ago or can a religious person advocate the use of hard drugs or violence to the President for *religious* reasons? The third level is the most controversial for it is in the practice of one's religious faith where one bumps directly against the sensitivities of one's neighbors and the larger society. How aberrant can the practices of a religious group be and still be tolerated? Our courts are continuously litigating on such matters and there seems to be little indication of a change in the near future.

The dynamic of identity formation tends
toward intolerant attitudes and behavior.

17

Going Beyond Tolerance A Developmental Task

Donald Freeman

What forms the attitudes and behavior of persons of any particular
faith toward persons of different faith traditions or toward persons
within the same faith tradition whose beliefs or practices differ?
Two formative influences upon such attitudes and behavior are (a)
the content of one's beliefs, and especially the implications of those
beliefs for the perspectives one properly takes towards persons of
other faiths and (b) the manner in which such beliefs and their implications are held, our concern in this essay.

The manner in which one holds one's beliefs may change while
the content remains basically the same; conversely, content may
change while the manner remains basically the same. One who
holds the doctrines of one faith literally may convert to a different
faith and hold its doctrines just as literally, or a person may shift
from a literal to a more metaphorical manner of holding the same
content of the same faith.

Stages of faith development are distinguishable, for descriptive
and analytical purposes, from stages or phases of other kinds of

development — moral, cognitive, social, biophysical, psychological, and the like — but the dynamics of development in any one of
these areas is affected in complex ways by other developmental
dynamics in the same living person. For instance, processes of social-
ization, individuation, and identity formation are likely to have
profound effects upon the manner in which faith is appropriated,
while the content and manner of one's faith may, in turn, have profound effects upon the formation of one's identity, etc.

Religious formation — the intentional nurture of faith — can
address the development of the manner in which one's faith is held
as much as the development of beliefs and practices. Religious
formation always does so, whether the manner is an intentional
consideration or not.

The remainder of this essay proposes a typology of attitudes and
behavior of persons toward others of differing views or practices;
presents Fowler's theory of faith development with an eye to such
attitudes and behavior;[1] and reviews several factors that are formative of such attitudes and behavior speculating on the implications
of these for religions.

Is "tolerance" the best — or only — possible goal?
A typology of attitudes and behavior

It is possible to lay out a continuum of attitudes and behavior
toward different views and practices ranging from great negativity
through indifference to great positivity, and to distinguish several
moments along that continuum in order to show that the opposite
poles share some significant similarities as well as great differences,
as will be shown by the diagram on the following page.

---

1. The most comprehensive and systematic presentation of this theory is in James W.
Fowler, *Stages of Faith: the Psychology of Human Development and the Quest for Meaning* (San Francisco: Harper & Row, 1981).

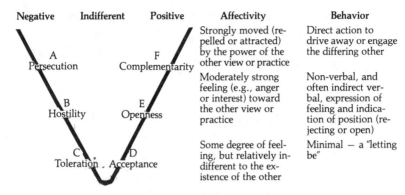

Negative	Indifferent	Positive	Affectivity	Behavior
			Strongly moved (repelled or attracted) by the power of the other view or practice	Direct action to drive away or engage the differing other
A Persecution		F Complementarity	Moderately strong feeling (e.g., anger or interest) toward the other view or practice	Non-verbal, and often indirect verbal, expression of feeling and indication of position (rejecting or open)
B Hostility		E Openness	Some degree of feeling, but relatively indifferent to the existence of the other	Minimal — a "letting be"
	C Toleration	D Acceptance		

Six attitudinal-behavioral stances along the continuum may be defined as follows:[2]

A. Persecution: Active effort to suppress, to prohibit, or to eradicate views and practices different from those of one's own group, and to enforce homogeneity and conformity within one's own group.

B. Hostility: Verbal and/or non-verbal communication that makes it clear that differing others are not wanted; indirect or passive-aggressive rather than direct action.

C. Toleration: The practice of "peaceful co-existence," but basically separatistic and non-associating. The implicit message is, "We don't need you and would rather that you were not around; but we will put up with you and leave you alone, so long as you leave us alone." If the rights of other groups are advocated, it is largely out of felt need to protect the rights of one's own group.

D. Acceptance: Affirming that differing others have the right to be around, and willingness to accomodate; positive regard for the apparent integrity of the other's views and practices, but little action to learn about them.

E. Openness: Relates to differing others and seeks to learn *about* (without expecting to learn *from*) their views and practices; supports social and cultural diversity and the kinds of legislation which protect it.

2. This construct is adapted from William L. Raker, "Affirming Varieties of Religious Experience: A Model for the Affirmation of Pluralism in the Local Church" (D. Min. dissertation, Lancaster Theological Seminary, 1981). Raker used the names, "persecution," "hostility," and "complementarity" as they are used above, but defined "tolerance" and "acceptance" more positively.

F. Complementarity: Conscious that, no matter how firmly convinced, one's own views and practices are imperfect; seeks mutual sharing with expectation of mutual benefit (learning *from* and not merely *about*), and advocates pluralism as an enrichment for all.

This essay advocates a climate more positive than tolerance: at least acceptance, perhaps openness, and ideally complementarity. It is also written with the awareness that in many situations tolerance is, indeed, the best that can be hoped for.

Developmental Stages In The Manner
In Which One Holds A Faith

Fowler, as previously mentioned, has constructed a theory which lays claim to a measure of descriptive accuracy about a sequence of six stages through which persons may develop in respect to faith. Fowler defines in broad and generic terms: "Faith is not always religious in its content or context.... Faith is a person's or group's way of moving into the force field of life. It is our way of finding coherence in and giving meaning to the multiple forces and relations that make up our lives. Faith is a person's way of seeing him- or herself in relation to others against a background of shared meaning and purpose.... We look for something to honor and respect that has the power to sustain our being."[3] Such a something may be an object, an idea, a cause, a person, a group, a life style, as well as a deity or being itself.

The description appears to hold true for persons of all faiths, religious and secular. The content of one's faith — the stories, images, norms of belief and practice, and personal experience of the sacred, the holy, or the ultimate — may affect the extent to and pace at which one develops, but not the sequence of stages, which seems to be constant. It is the form — or, as I have been calling it, the manner — of faith which undergoes the developmental changes described by this theory, and these changes may or may not involve major changes in the content as such.

Movement from one stage to the next is not guaranteed. For instance, apparently few persons proceed to the sixth stage; perhaps

3. *Stages of Faith*, pp. 4, 5.

even a majority do not move beyond the third. There is a tendency to "settle in" ("equilibrate") at whatever stage one may be in, although life circumstances and experiences have a tendency to unsettle persons again some time in the passage of years. The stages are not simply successive: each stage incorporates one's previous stages, but in a new perspective. Once a new perspective is established, it is not really possible to retreat to a previous stage, even though one can participate in it. But a major shift from one faith content to another, as in a conversion, may entail a kind of quick retracing of the steps again from pre-stage or Stage 1 forward.

Following is a summary presentation of the stages a described by Fowler, with a brief characterization of the manner in which a faith is embraced in each:

0 — Undifferentiated. Key issues appear to be the development of basic trust and of interpersonal mutuality.

1 — Intuitive-projective. The contents of faith, affective as well as cognitive, are appropriated from "significant others" by observation and imitation, and related to one another imaginatively. Relations among stories, beliefs, practices and feelings are not fixed but fluid. Images and their accompanying affects are often profoundly powerful throughout one's life as vivid memories either recalled or suppressed — especially images and feelings of objects of awe and fear: death, sex, taboos. Long-lasting images may be formed of, and deep affective responses made toward persons and groups who trusted significant others indicate are to be avoided, shunned, loathed, feared, distrusted, or the like.

2 — Mythic-literal. The fluidity of imagination in stage 1 is displaced by more fixed connections provided by story, drama and myth. Beliefs, symbols, moral rules, and attitudes are appropriated in a naively literal manner. Persons and groups who have views and practices which differ from those of one's own significant others are generally and easily characterized by rather undifferentiated stereotypical images: labels such as right/wrong, good/bad, friend/enemy are uncritically accepted and often applied with a consistency and persistence which may seem from other perspectives to be cruel and vicious. It is a pre-personal stage, a stage of rules, orderliness, deeds, and their enforcers and doers (often heroes) rather than personalities.

3 — Synthetic-conventional. This is the stage of personalities, where meanings reside in the warmth of relationships among the persons of depth and feeling who constitute one's world of significance. Deity, if a part of one's faith, is generally personalized and rational. Values, beliefs, symbols, rules and practices are owned deeply, described articulately, and defended passionately, because they are perceived to be held by "everyone" and are expected by the significant others who have authority by office or respect; they form an aggregate the consistency of which is *felt* more than conceptualized — that is, they form a tacit system which does not normally, as a system, become an object of reflection. These values not only express and symbolize the sacred, they *are*, in a real sense, the sacred because they participate in it. People who are perceived to be at variance with them are also often seen as threats to them, and are either pressured to conform or made objects of suspicion, if not hostility. Variant groups are stereotyped and treated in the same way as variant individuals. Paradoxically, however, specific interpersonal relationships are often established across group lines, as if the persons were not really connected with their value systems; hence the cliche, "Some of my best friends are N's" (N's being a suspect or rejected group), may be honestly descriptive from a Stage 3 perspective.

¾ — Transition. Although this occurs between stages 3 and 4, it can best be understood after reading about Stage 4. See below.

4 — Individuative-reflexive. The religious system is now recognized as such and elaborated critically and conceptually; symbols and images are demythologized, their meanings translated into concepts and propositions. Feelings may be even more powerfully present than before, but it is the consistency of the system which is the honored object of consciousness. Moreover, the individual now takes personal responsibility for the choice of a faith — not because it is expected of one, but because one is personally convinced; and as one personally understands it, whether or not anyone else understands it the same way. Faith has taken on a consistent and ideological quality in respect of both belief and practice. A person in Stage 4 is acutely aware of differences with other worldviews, acutely critical of them, but well able to apprehend the other

persons who hold such world-views in terms of their personal qualities as much as their ideologies.

The transition from Stage 3 to Stage 4 may occur in a partial and incomplete way. Fowler identifies two types of protracted transition between these two stages. In the first, the person has become critically — and often painfully — aware of the relativity of her/his inherited world view, but continues to rely on external sources of authority. Such a person may seek refuge from relativism in a new absolutism, such as the absolute truth of a dogmatic system, the absolute authority of a charismatic leader, or the absolute orthopraxy of a committed group — or, most often, some combination of these. In the second type of transition between stages 3 and 4, the person — or often an independent group has ceased relying on conventional authority and taken deliberate ownership of her/his/their values, but still simply assumes those values rather than subjecting them to criticism.

5 — Conjunctive Faith is held in a very paradoxical manner: Its most powerful meanings are at once more fully appreciated and yet recognized to be relative and partial. The ideological purity of Stage 4 has been defeated by the undeniable complexities of life — Fowler calls it "the sacrament of defeat.[4] The fullness of the affective self is now equally honored and integrated with the cognitive self:

> Alive to paradox and the truth in apparent contradictions, this stage strives to unify opposites in mind and experience. It generates and maintains vulnerability to the strange truths of those who are "other." Ready for closeness to that which is different and threatening to self and outlook (including new depths of experience in spirituality and religious revelation), this stage's commitment to justice is freed from the confines of tribe, class, religious community or nation.[5]

6 — Universalizing. Since this stage is so rare, Fowler has based his characterization of it on theological more than empirical grounds. He is convinced that essential to the content of Stage 6 is a vision of the "ultimate environment" as inclusive of all being, and to its manner the disposition both to love life and to hold it loosely; that is, to give oneself totally to the imperatives of universal love and justice,

4. Fowler, *Stages*, p. 198

5. Ibid.

heedless of labels, boundaries and limiting distinctions, and heedless of the consequences to one's own being or well-being. His list of persons who have probably come to Stage 6 includes Gandhi, Dietrich Bonhoeffer, Abraham Heschel, Dag Hammerskjöld, Martin Luther King, Jr., and Mother Theresa.[6] The early stages of the process are conducive to hostility to other traditions. Stage 1 can become a time for the formation of deepseated negative feelings toward certain kinds of people and groups, insofar as the young child senses the fears or other feelings of primal or highly significant others. Similar appropriation of feelings may occur in Stages 2, 3, and the ¾ transition. It is not until Stage 4 proper that the tyranny of such feelings is likely to be critically addressed.

Stages 4 and 5 are characterized by progressively more positive attitudes toward other groups and persons whose views and practices differ from one's own. Even though the content of a faith may entail or imply hostile attitude and behavior or other forms of intolerance as normative, the manner in which the faith is held fosters, in full Stage 4, toleration and perhaps acceptance, and, in Stage 5, acceptance and openness if not complementarity.

From these trends comes one of our basic conclusions: One of the ways to improve the climate for a plurality of religious traditions is to engage intentionally in the development of faith beyond the uncritically socialized Stages 1 — ¾ to the critical personal owership which characterizes Stages 4 and 5.

From developmental theory comes also the sobering thought which Immanuel Kant advanced two centuries ago concerning the idea of moral progress of the human race: Every time a human being is born, the whole process starts anew. Hence this means of improving the climate is not a once-and-for-all effort, but one which must be kept at persistently.

Persons in stages 2, 3, and ¾ are formed by normative statements of their faiths precisely because they accept givens of their faith uncritically. Persons in Stage 4 are also — not because they accept uncritically, but because they value normative statements, especially when they are consistent with the belief system. In the literatures of

6. Ibid. p. 201

most enduring religious traditions are to be found such normative statements about the appropriate attitudes and behavior of their faithful adherents toward other religious traditions and the adherents to those traditions. Some of these statements may call for, or simply imply the appropriateness of, persecution or hostility. In my own tradition, Christianity, every one of the six attitudinal-behavioral stances along the previously defined continuum can be justified with statements from the written tradition. It is therefore not possible to characterize Christianity by any of these stances, although both of the extremes, persecution and complementarity, are less frequently to be found than the others. The normative statements which are formally operative on a particular Christian individual are thus to be found not in the tradition as a whole, but in a particular sub-tradition, the literature which that group accepts as authoritative, and the accepted interpretations of that literature. The same is probably true of all other religious traditions which have had extensive spread or history. Be that as it may: It is likely that formal normative statements of any tradition have less formative influence on its believers than the other three factors.

Two types of personal experiences may be especially formative in the process of faith development, in addition to the internalization of group norms mentioned above. One is the development of a relationship of mutual respect and appreciation with a person or persons of differing views or practices. When it is an isolated instance for a person in Stage 3, it may not be experienced as incongruous with a negative stance toward the group of which that other person is a member, because it is the interpersonal rather than the group relationship which is perceived to be primary. But when a person in Stage 3 has a succession of similar experiences of encounter with persons whose integrity and differentness cannot be denied, they may accumulate to a critical point where Stage 3 faith is no longer viable and transition toward Stage 4 is virtually forced. So, too, a person in Stage 4 may find it impossible to account for such integrity and meaning and be pushed toward Stage 5. Exposure to pluralism is itself an agent of faith development if it involves interpersonal and intellectual depth and not merely superficiality.

The other type of personal experience, which is also often an occasion for development from one stage of faith to another, is the negative experience of suffering, disillusionment, tragedy, bereavement, rejection, or terror. One may find a Stage 2 — or 3 or 4 — faith inadequate to sustain a sense of meaning in life and move into a time of transition and, hopefully, into the next stage.

Intrapersonal needs are a final factor shaping attitudes toward other traditions. The development of a sense of identity is one of the most powerful of needs, and it begins during infancy, if not earlier. In general terms, we often identify ourselves and our group by who we are *not* more specifically than by who we *are*: We are not like *them*. Faith Stage 2 contributes to identity formation by connecting the person with a larger story, the story owned by the faith community. In faith Stage 3, identity is further confirmed by relationships and by the articulation of the values important to the network of interrelationships which is at the heart of one's group or community: one gains identity by sharing beliefs and practices, values and feelings. Protracted transitional Stage ¾, in either of its forms, also continues to draw identity from eternal relationships — to an authority, or to a group and its ways. It is with full Stage 4 that identity becomes a more internally-grounded reality — often relying on relationship to an explicit belief system, but one which is one's own. And by Stage 5 that inward sense of identity is sufficiently secure that the openness to different others is no longer so prohibitively threatening.

It has long been asserted that social identity is congealed by either the reality or the myth of a common enemy; that is, social identity is aided by clear distinction from what it is not. There is in this phenomenon of identity by distinction a natural ground for negative attitudes and behavior toward any others from which one and one's group are distinguished. This, then, is another disturbing conclusion of this essay: that the dynamic of identity formation by reference to and distinction from others tends, unless taken under deliberate control, toward intolerant attitudes and behavior toword those others from whom one is distinguished. Intolerance is not a necessary, but perhaps almost an inevitable, byproduct of human development itself. But development need not stop there, as this essay has already asserted: a more complete development can be to — and beyond — tolerance.

Life is an abundant offering and it is
a force that lifts us up out of our ideas
and opinions and propels us into action,
into commitment, into involvement.

18

Singing the Song of Life

Helen Glassmann

As a 43-year-old human being, I have learned to appreciate and
enjoy my work, my marriage, my children, and myself. Yet, I have
many expectations and ideas of how I would like things to be, how
I would arrange and organize my life and life on earth if I could.
When I bump into the reality of how things are in contrast to my
hopes and expectations, I bump into fear and disappointment.

I think that it is this fear and disappointment that make us dis-
agree so disagreeably; I feel that it is our very personal fears and
disappointments, not our strong religious identities, that isolate us
from one another and I sense that self-righteousness in all human
action — not only politics — is in direct relationship to our fears
and disappointments.

Fear of loss is overpowering at times for us. We're like tadpoles
living in a small puddle drying up in the sun. Time and life is short
and very fragile. We're all familiar with someone in mid-life crisis
who, realizing that youth and beauty and strength are fading, has
one or many affairs to convince themselves that attractiveness and
youth and vigor are intact. We all have experienced in our personal
and work relationships the fear of loss of love or respect and, most

frightening of all, loss of control. To be in control, we have organized and arranged our lives in a thousand different ways depending on our personalities. Control for some of us is marriage, for others it is being uncommitted and single; for some it is a steady job, for others it is free-lancing; for some it is a regular and committed schedule, for others it is always leaving things open. And then there is disappointment and the sadness and anger that it engenders. Disappointment that our parents were not as loving and supportive as we would have wished them to be; that we, as parents, are not so perfect; that our children are at times so trying and demanding. We wish that we could have accomplished more in our work, been more creative, more or less aggressive, less overworked. And we sometimes worry about our faith, the fervor of our religious commitment and practices and so we criticize ourselves and our religious leaders. We and they are not good enough, kind enough, giving enough, pure enough.

But life and reality seem to mosey along independent and irrespective of our ideas and values. To me, life is a fulfilled and total realization of all of our feelings and energies and commitment. Life is an abundant offering and it is a force that lifts us up out of our ideas and opinions and propels us into action, into commitment, into involvement. We may think we are committed or we may think we are disillusioned, but we are life and life is us and we are constantly participating and offering — anew — anew — anew. And every new moment is a new creation of life's offering. It is your offering, my offering, his offering, our offering. And most of all it is a present offering. Here and now is the most powerful time of our lives. Here and now is the culmination of dynamic functioning of the efforts of all creation.

I may think that the only way for my beliefs to be true is to disqualify the beliefs of others, to assume that they are superior to other views, or to universalize other views and say that we are saying the same thing. However, I feel that my views are not the only qualifying views, not the superior views and not the same views as those of others. I feel that all of these views are radically interdependent — that truth is decentralized and inextricably bound up with the particular life it participates in and that all of these truths are the harmonious functioning of the one body of life.

The thirteenth century Zen master Dogen Zenji says:

Life is for example like a man sailing in a boat. Although he sets a sail, steers his course and poles the boat along, the boat carries him. By sailing in the boat he makes it what the boat is . . . . at such a time there is nothing but the world of the boat. . . . Hence I make life what it is; life makes me what I am. In riding the boat one's body and mind, the self and the world are together the dynamic function of the boat. The entire earth and the whole empty sky are in company with the boats vigorous exertion. Such is the I that is life, the life that is I.

And:

Not a single moment, not a single thing exists that does not co-work with life. Not a single event, not a single mind exists that does not take part in life.

Jesus said, "The Kingdom of Heaven is at hand." And the Buddha said as an expression of his enlightenment experience: "How wonderful! How wonderful! Everything just as it is is the enlightened way." The essence of the certainty of enlightenment is *not knowing.* This calls for a complete and accepting openness to life as it comes up. Christians call it poverty; that poverty of mind and spirit not rich in ideas and opinions about how life should be. This enlightenment is a deep acceptance of the human situation as absolutely particular. Momentarily this "I" standing here sees a view of "now" and then, in the next moment, a changed "I," changed by the previous moment, sees "just now." And it goes on. A willingness, an openness to the absolute uncertainty of "who and what" is knowing and understanding what is — this is the pillar of Zen strength and life. I cannot say it is a view of life as inexorable process. It is, rather, a realization of no view — a radical commitment to life here and now as it arises, as I in my particularity experience it.

We as humans have particular kinds of physical bodies and mental equipment. It is equipment that grows and changes, it accumulates knowledge and ideas and sorts, categorizes, forgets and remembers. We don't expect to realize our lives as flies do — we don't have faceted eyes and wings. We don't expect to realize our lives as dolphins do — our facility in water is not so great. Our appreciation of the importance of color and smell is certainly not that a bee. While it's easy to recognize and see differences of understanding and perception between humans and animals, most of us find it much more difficult to appreciate that each human being is unique. Each is an unparalleled combination of intuitive ideas, feelings and sensation capacity. Each has unique heredity, religious and cultural background and understanding. How can a friend, neighbor, cousin, American, earthling or other life form appreciate or understand as I do. How can this "I" appreciate now in the same way as it did at age 5 or 17 or as it will at 72? Do I want it to be the same appreciation?

My life is absolutely dependent on the life offering that each person and creature makes standing where he or she is at this time. I love tomatoes, especially garden fresh ones, but if we're all going to be offering tomatoes, I'm going to end up with an upset stomach. If one truly feels that this is God's world, then the kingdom of heaven is at hand; if one as a humanist feels a radical involvment and commitment to life, then the issue is not an idea or opinion of what's happening. None of the expressions of right or wrong or of success or failure mean anything. The issue is living fully in whatever way one understands and feels. A journalist in Calcutta once questioned Mother Theresa about the endless labor and utter hopelessness of the sick and the dying in India. She was totally baffled by his question. "My business is not to succeed," she said, "my business is to keep the faith." Her life is committed to life as it is. It's an nonjudgemental and utterly radical committment to life as it is. She does not set herself up to judge God and his ways or the organization of matter and energy. Her business is not to recreate the world in her own image. Her business is to accept and nurture God's life and world in the best way she knows how.

I believe that each of us offers the very best that he or she can to this life. The stomach produces enzymes and the heart pumps blood. I could say that we should all be hearts and pump blood or that we should all be the one thousand hands and arms of the Buddhist image of Kannon, the Bodhisattva of Compassion. But we aren't. Some of us are elbows, shoulder blades, kidneys, and tendons.

While I do not agree with many of the policies of the present administration (and I write letters to my representatives about how I feel), I accept and appreciate that they are willing to be involved in brokering complicated human relationships. I find the intricate causes and effects of our world so amazingly complicated that I am never sure that the causes I support lead to the effects I desire or whether the causes I dislike lead to effects that I appreciate. I do feel, however, that just as it arises, it is my life and the life of all creation.

The limit of religious tolerance, I feel, is many times a measure of the fear people feel in the face of the unknown. Somehow something will seem to be more true if all the people I know or run into seem to do and think as I do. My feeling is that intolerance is fear of life and of God's world.

There lived in Palestine in the early part of our century a very great rabbi, a rabbi so great that ultra orthodox Jews and secularists felt that he was *their* rabbi and understood and appreciated *their* views. And they all supported him and so he was elected chief rabbi of Israel. Rabbi Abraham Isaac Kook wrote this song:

There is one who sings the song of his own life, and in himself he finds everything, his full spiritual satisfaction.

There is another who sings the song of his people. He leaves the circle of his own individual self, because he finds it without sufficient breadth, without an idealistic basis.... He aspires toward the heights and he attaches himself with a gentle love to the whole community of Israel. Together with her he sings her songs. He feels grieved in her afflications and delights in her hopes. He contemplates noble and pure thoughts about her past and her future and probes with love and wisdom her inner spiritual essence.

There is another who reaches toward more distant realms and he goes beyond the boundary of Israel to sing the song of man. His spirit extends to the wider vistas of the majesty of man, generally, and his noble essence. He aspires toward man's general goal and looks forward toward his higher perfection. From this source of life he draws the subjects of his meditation and study, his aspirations and his visions.

Then there is one who rises toward wider horizons until he links himself with all existence, with all God's creatures with all worlds, and he sings his song with all of them. It is of one such as this that tradition has said that whoever sings a portion of song each day is assured of having a share in the world to come.

And then there is one who rises with all these songs in one ensemble, and they all join their voices. Together they sing their songs with beauty, each one lends vitality and life to the other. They are sounds of joy and gladness, sounds of jubilation and celebration, sounds of ecstacy and holiness.

The song of self, the song of the people, the song of man, the song of the world all merge in him at all times, in every hour.

And this full comprehensiveness rises to become the song of holiness, the song of God, the song of Israel, in its strength and beauty in its full authenticity and greatness. The name "Israel" stands for "shir el" the song of God. It is a simple song, a twofold song, a threefold song, and a fourfold song. It is the Song of Songs of Solomon, Shlomo, which means peace or wholeness. It is the song of the King in whom is wholeness.

Rabbi Kook was a very special man; he realized this song of life. Sometimes we don't see it and we're sad or angry or contentious. Sometimes we do see it and we're uplifted. But whether we don't see it and are sad or whether we see it and are uplifted, I believe it is the song of life.

> I urge atheism as a program for consciously
> stepping out of tribal patternings for at least
> some of the time and for experimenting with
> non-religious forms of building community.

19

Stepping Out of the Circle: Overcoming Tribal Identities

Naomi R. Goldenberg

The question of who we are is never asked independently of social requirements. And, further, the answer we give the question is always selective. Who I am is always both a matter of who I say I am and who you let me be. Because we are all continually constructing one another, our identities have some flexibility. This conviction makes me optimistic.

The flexibility of "identity" is something I've learned from my triple roles of Jew, feminist and atheist. I like playing these parts and am glad that they are possible stances available to me in contemporary culture. Let me explain what I think each perspective has to offer.

I grew up as one of the only Jewish kids in a predominantly Christian neighborhood. I thus encountered a lot of crosses around other children's necks. I always saw these images as stop signs. To me they said "Go away, this means you. I am a cross around a Christian neck and I am worn to keep people like you at a safe distance." As a child, I grew up feeling hurt and rejected by crosses, crucifixes and most all other Christian paraphernalia. (Except Christmas trees. Those wonderful, essentially pagan things never made me feel unwelcome). That feeling of rejection still lingers. I cannot look at a cross without feeling some sadness and some anger. This feeling of exclusion is also present in a smaller degree when anyone wears a cross verbally — that is, when anyone says "I am a Christian."

As a child, my defense against the rejection posed by crosses could have been to don a Jewish star. I had several in my jewelry box — including my favorite, a star my father had found lying in a German street after the war. But I never felt comfortable wearing a Jewish star. Perhaps I didn't want to be singled out as someone so very different. Being crossless was hard enough.

Even when I went to high school and had a majority of Jews in my class, I still didn't join many of them in wearing a star. Now my sense of difference was the result of economic factors. The Jews with whom I went to high school were generally the children of well-to-do professionals. My family was more lower class. Even though I was certainly "accepted" by my classmates, I felt the economic inequalities as a vague sense of not really belonging to my Jewish peer group.

The result of these early experiences of exclusion give me what some call a "lack of a strong sense of Jewish identity." Which simply means that I don't exhibit the "Jewish identity" that the people who say this would like me to show. And yet, I feel very Jewish — very comfortable about being Jewish in the way it means to me.

My experience of being relatively poor and Jewish within a wealthy Jewish social group in a predominantly Christian environment did a good thing for me. It gave me the perspective of an outsider. (And this, of course, has been one important experience of many Jews at many other points in history.) An outsider is someone who, because she feels outside a social structure, can see some of the ways "outsides" and "insides" are constructed. My history of exclusion from both the Christian world and from a part of the Jewish world puts me in a position to be able to articulate some very useful things.

Now, at this point, a certain sensitivity to psychoanalytic truth urges me to suspect what I have just said. I sound a bit smug and a bit triumphant. I am turning my past experience of social rejection into a good thing partially in order to defend myself from the pain of it. The sense of being prophetic often arises in people who want to compensate for feeling socially out-of-place. But, having said this, I still believe that anyone who is aware of their own experience of confusion about identity has some important things to teach us about what we call the sense of self. Since we are all somewhat "confused" about who we are, we can learn from each other that identity is not a simple given. One's identity or rather one's identities are always conditioned by past history and present circumstance.

One way I am conscious of myself as a Jew is as a critic, as an iconoclast, as someone eternally suspicious of what is going on. I feel there is a lot of truth in Isaac Bashevis Singer's remark that "Jews are people who can't sleep and who don't want anyone else to sleep either." That description applies to a part of me.[1]

My particular sense of Jewishness made me eager to learn from the feminist movement. The experience of sisterhood as a community of outsiders, and the philosophy of feminism as the reflections of outsiders seemed very real and necessary for me. The women's movement has, I feel, helped me to better understand how human difference translates into social script.

Feminism has let me see how we are a species that exaggerates the biological differences which do exist between the sexes. Difference between male and female genitalia become signs that proscribe different social roles for men and women. Many feminists have insisted that women could do what men do — and, I think they are right. Other feminists have insisted that, even though we women can do much of what men do, we still are "different." I think they are right too.[2]

The continual feminist revery on human difference — how it is at the same time artificial and yet not to be ignored — can teach us all, men and women, that we are an essentially heterogeneous

1. Recently, I've been overjoyed to see that a group of sleep-disturbers have started a magazine called *Tikkun* — a *Jewish Critique of Politics, Culture and Society*. It is becoming an expression of that critical voice that always expresses worry about social injustice — a voice with which I identify as a Jew.

2. Sandra Harding, "The Instability of the Analytical Categories of Feminist Theory," *Signs*, Vol. 11, No. 4, (Summer 1986), pp. 645-664.

species, teeming with possibilities of feeling, behavior, action and inaction. Cultures — whether of gender, nationality or religion — differ from each other according to which human possibilities they permit and which they discourage.

Feminist theorists like Luce Irigaray have suggested that perhaps our conventional sense of what it means to have an identity arises from a particularly male sense of body.[3] Men, Irigaray suggests, are obsessed with keeping their bodies intact, with not being cut off or castrated from parts of themselves. This concern has led men to create social groupings which maintain a rigid sense of territory. Men in groups are always issuing orders which say — "This land is mine; these women are mine; these men take orders from me." Male identity is built around a concept of the tribe and its territory as being the jealously guarded parts of a masculine body. If man B's tribe settles on man A's land and has access to A's women, A will feel diminished, as if he were cut off from a part of his own body.

I think we see the male need to aggrandize masculine bodies in the custom of giving wives and children male surnames. A man can never have the same certainty about connection to a child as can the woman who gave birth to that child. His worry over whether or not that baby really is a part of him is expressed in his insistence on giving both the woman and the child his name. In order to allay this male insecurity, men construct a social order that insists on giving *their* women and children a clear sense of tribal allegiance and loyalty.

Think of this for a moment in regard to religion. Most all of us here identify our religions along the lines of male tribal hierarchy. We follow a single male God, a single male leader, or a group of male leaders. Christ, Moses, Yahweh, the Reverend Moon, Buddha, Confucius, the Church fathers, the rabbis, the priests, the college of cardinals. We have been taught that these male figures should serve as models or teachers for the proper methods of organizing our lives. We follow male ways. We live with those who are like us because they follow the same male ways. By doing this to the dif-

---

3. Luce Irigaray, *This Sex Which Is Not One*, trans. Catherine Porter (Ithaca, N.Y.: Cornell University Press, 1985).

fering degrees in which we do it, aren't we behaving as members of male-headed tribes? And, perhaps, aren't we allowing the male obsession with bodily integrity and tribal order to limit our associations with each other — to limit the ways in which we might live? I think we should at least be asking these questions.

Women, says Irigaray, perhaps, do not need to insist so long and hard on a single "identity." In fact, she thinks that female pleasure may well involve a sense of connection to many physical and social experiences. The question of what women want always must be answered in the plural. Female "desire" is variable.

Here I want to underline my conviction that even if Irigaray is right about the dominant oneness of men's desire and the plurality of women's wants, I do feel that both possibilities exist for both sexes. We have, until now, largely scripted our world around one kind of male will — the will to incorporate as tribes. We could arrange societies around less unitary patterns. Perhaps male desire, male will, has some plural possibilities that the feminist movement can encourage.

There are feminists who reject Irigaray's suggestion that there are any characteristics such as a capacity for diversity which we can label as essentially female. They believe that the feminist call for radical pluralism is simply the result of women's growing political sophistication. If we do not learn to relate to such other across differences, say these feminists, we may soon have no world at all. Thus, new ways of organizing the human community must be found — ways that transcend the old system of competitive tribal allegiances thought up by men. Feminist theorist Audre Lorde advances the argument like this:

> The future of our earth may depend upon the ability of all women to identify and develop new definitions of power and new patterns of relating across difference. The old definitions have not served us, nor the earth that supports us.
>
> ... we have, built into all of us, old blueprints of expectation and response, old structures of oppression, and these must be altered at the same time as we alter the living conditions which are a result of those structures. For the master's tools will never dismantle the master's house. [4]

4. Audre Lorde, *Sister/Outsider*, (Trumansburg, N.Y.: The Crossing Press), p. 123.

As I see it, a grand mission for feminism is to dismantle the master's house and to set about building new houses for both women and men. Feminism demands a thorough examination of all prejudices, all stereotypes and all enforced separations of human beings along male tribal lines. As a practice, as a discourse, as a revolutionary strategy, feminism aims to transform the human community by questioning the established social groupings and by making us all realize how much we are implicated in the fate of one another.

Feminism, of course, is not the only force working to break down national and tribal allegiances. The artificiality of national boundaries soon becomes apparent to anyone thinking seriously about world hunger, or environmental problems, or nuclear arms. The fact that one crop is being planted in one part of the third world for export to North America often means that local farmers no longer cultivate products for domestic use. The local population can become dependent on external food supplies. Thus North American desires for consumption affect the third world.[5]

Pollution, like the food supply, is also an issue which dissolves national boundaries. In Canada, where I live now, pollutants from U. S. industry get in the atmosphere and rain down on northern lakes and rivers. Canadian water then becomes clear, free of algae and indeed free of all life. There are no sovereign states in relation to an issue like pollution.

So too does the anxiety about nuclear war urge us to change our traditional views about separate nations, states and tribes. Jonathan Schell, in the *Fate of the Earth* urges us all to rethink the system of strong national identities that has brought about the ever-present threat of nuclear war. Loyalty to single nations is the simple extension of loyalty to single tribes. It is a practice which can no longer offer us security (if ever it did).

I realize that there is something very cozy about the tribe. Even if "tribes" are basically expressions of masculine fantasies because they have been around for a long time they do offer us a sense of order and definition. But, I believe with Schell that the familial sense of warmth is a false security in this twentieth century. Developing

5. Peggy Cleveland, "Mothering the Earth: A Metaphor for Sustainability", unpublished paper presented November 25th at the 1985 meeting of the American Academy of Religion in Anaheim, California.

our collective capacities to feel empathy, involvement and identity beyond our particular tribe is more essential for us now.

Now let me come back to religion. I think that the breakdown of tribal organization can be helped by a certain degree of atheism in the world. I can get downright messianic about atheism. All the papal documents which I have read about the scourge of atheism seem to me very misguided. Atheists are, in fact, essential to a better world.

Atheism is, in fact, "peopleism." And, since it is only people who pose the greatest threat to people and only people who can save people, atheism reflects a reality. "Now that we can nuke God," says a friend of mine, "we had better think seriously about each other." The concept of God, I find, downplays the concept of people. It lets us kid ourselves about what we are doing and encourages us to disguise human agency.

Many concepts of God mystify our tribal patterns with notions that a group's behavior derives from God. Many concepts of God allow us to disguise our own subjectivity or the subjectivity of clerical rulers as "divine will." I think we will be much safer if we insist on understanding how it is that we human beings have made our history, our ideas, and each other than if we pretend that there is some sort of supernatural agency at work outside of ourselves.

I suggest that it is the moral duty of every person — religious or non-religious — to live at least part of her or his life as either an atheist or a polytheist. I urge atheism as a program for consciously stepping out of tribal patternings for at least some of the time and for experimenting with non-religious forms of building community. Perhaps some of the good things that have chiefly been available within religious traditions can flourish elsewhere. For example, the inspiration and sustenance to be found in some mystical practices could perhaps be fostered in secular groups.

If commitment to secular groups is not possible for the theist who has derived much nourishment from a sense of religious identity, then I suggest that all theists live part of their lives as polytheists. A polytheist would be obliged to acquaint herself or himself and her or his children with a few religious perspectives in order to encourage the capacity for empathy with people seen as "others."

Although atheism is, in a sense, my calling, I do feel that having a religious affiliation is not in itself a harmful thing. There is nothing wrong with being a Christian or a Jew or a Moslem or a Hindu as long as these identities are not used as walls to being or becoming anything else or anyone else. But if being a Christian or a Jew becomes a program which sets up rigid priorities of concern for the particular group considered one's own, then there is something wrong.

If there can be said to be a "spiritual" goal for these times, I think it makes some sense to describe it in the way Freud described the goal of psychoanalysis. "Where id was, there ego shall be," he once wrote.[6] Or, in other words, where "it" was there "I" shall be. We need to expand our senses of "I-ness" — our sense of the range of human emotion and experience so that we can all better tolerate diversity. But tolerate is a tricky word. There is an arm's length quality about it — a refusal to interact. True toleration expands the ego, the sense of who "I" am. True toleration is also somewhat threatening because it usually means that "I" have to change. Despite the fear, we must, I think, let ourselves affect one another. "I am who I am," says Audre Lorde, "doing what I came to do, acting upon you like a drug or a chisel to remind you of your meness, as I discover you in myself."[7]

---

6. Sigmund Freud, *The Standard Edition of the Complete Psychological Works of Sigmund Freud*, 24 vols., ed. James Strachey (London: Hogarth Press, 1953-1974), vol. XXII, p. 80.

7. Audre Lorde, p. 147.

**Circles That
Interconnect**

> We hope our experience will prove . . .
> that the need to keep us in and others
> out will disappear. The mutual exchange
> and contribution will be so fruitful that
> we will have to open the gates for friendly
> comings and goings until, eventually,
> the demarcation will disappear . . .

20

Walls, Fences, and Homes for the Homeless

Sister Joan Kirby

MENDING WALL
by Robert Frost

. . . . "Good fences make good neighbors."
Spring is the mischief in me, and I wonder
If I could put a notion in his head:
"Why do they make good neighbors? Isn't it
Where there are cows? But there are no cows.
Before I built a wall I'd ask to know
What I was walling in or walling out,
And to whom I was like to give offence.
Something there is that doesn't love a wall,
That wants it down." I could say "Elves" to him,
But its not elves exactly, and I'd rather
He said it for himself. I see him there
Bringing a stone grasped firmly by the top
In each hand, like an old stone-savage armed.

He moves in darkness as it seems to me,
Not of woods only, and the shade of trees.
He will not go behind his father's saying,
And he likes having thought of it so well
He says again, "Good fences make good neighbors."[1]

We are engaged in an ongoing argument at Homes for the Homeless (an Interfaith Project of the Cathedral of St. John the Divine) over a fence at the Family Inn in Queens. This is a very large Inn for 250 families. Teenagers, adolescents and young children will raise the population to 700. The site is in an Air Cargo area behind Kennedy Airport but it is 4-5 blocks away from a community of homeowners who violently oppose the intrusion of homeless in their neighborhood. Many homeowners have been demonstrating against our use of the former Holiday Inn for homeless families.

The property is large and open. Many questions confront us. Should we leave it without boundaries with no barriers to access and egress? Should we put up a fence to enclose the play areas for little children, for teenage basketball games? Or, should we enclose the entire property providing access only through one entrance (and exit through the same)? If we fence it, how high should the fence be — 6 feet, 8 feet, 10 feet? What is the purpose of the fence? To keep our families from roaming all over the neighborhood — where they are not welcome? Or, is the fence to keep out the demonstrators, i.e. the opposition? Why do we put up fences anyway? To delineate what belongs to us, to set a boundary.... And, why do we move to the next level and make a wall that is impenetrable? "Something there is that doesn't love a wall," but "good fences make good neighbors" according to Frost's traditional wisdom. In fact, Robert Frost's poem has helped to settle our long argument; good fences make good neighbors. We have definitely rejected a wall. It would give a message opposite to that which we want to communicate. It would speak of separation, threat, and would invite a surprise attack by wall scalers. For the time being, we will make a good

1. Copyright 1930, 1939, © 1969 by Holt, Rinehart and Winston, Inc. Copyright © 1967 by Lesley Frost Ballantine. Reprinted from THE POETRY OF ROBERT FROST edited by Edward Connery Lathem, by permission of Henry Holt and Company, Inc.

fence, not a wall, and we will work to eliminate the needs for walls. We want to create a more humane, more compassionate transitional home for our families, one which will empower rather than depress them. We hope our experience will prove, as it has in the South Bronx (at our first Interfaith Family Inn), that the need to keep us in and others out will disappear. The mutual exchange and contribution may be so fruitful that we will have to open the gates for friendly comings and goings until, eventually, the demarcation will disappear between our families and the surrounding community. We will become part of an enlarged, expanded community.

The topic for this conference asks me to build another fence — to design it, to decide how high, to set its limits; I have had a similar internal argument over this other fence. "Something there is that doesn't love a wall." That was my initial reaction. There should be almost no limit to tolerance. We are all believers; that is the important issue. How and why would we establish boundaries that keep others out and ourselves in? Yet, boundaries turn out to be healthy limits. Educators are clear about the need for boundaries for growing children — the worst thing is to yield the limits. Therapists tell us that our sense of self comes through our personal identity, our separateness from others. Healthy relationships are those which allow for intimacy and are not symbiotic.

Religious tolerance sets limits. Tolerance implies a certain reserve — it lacks warmth, welcome and affection, but it separates us for healthy growth. That is good. Limits acknowledge our finitude; we cannot manage the infinite. We need a religious home just as the families at our Inns need a home. But, though fences make good neighbors, it is not healthy to protect religious security within a high and impenetrable wall. If your search for God is a threat to my faith, then that sets a wall between us and that is not good.

Thus, reasonable limits serve a healthy *temporary* purpose. Inside the fence I have my Church — Roman Catholic Church, as worshipper, teacher, healer:

The Church offers worship, intercedes for us with God, leads us into His Holy Place.

The Church is teacher — of doctrine, of ethics, of just relations among people.

And the Church is the official Healer, qualified to forgive sin and to mediate reconcilation.

These are the not insignificant functions performed within the Church, but at the heart of the Christian Church tradition is the Pascal mystery, meaning the surrender of power. The Son of God, Christ, surrendered power and prestige. He avoided solidarity with a group of religious insiders. He went outside the walls, in order to express his compassion and love for the poor and oppressed. Love, which is the surrender of power, and a mysterious regaining of power, is the heart of Christianity. Compassion is the motivating power, and Jesus seems to have had a mysterious preference for the poor and cast-outs of society. Love induced Christ, the Son of God, to undergo death; and love enpowered His resurrection — His transformation.

This is the model at the heart of Christianity. Love accepts, even embraces, death. It goes into darkness with a mysterious trust in the efficacy of dying, and, love enables rebirth and transformation.

The institutional Church teaches this cycle, celebrates the cycle in our liturgical worship. Yet, the institutional Church resists the cycle in its own institutional life. Our buildings, our schools, our churches, our instinct to preserve the tradition make us cling to what we have built and resist the inevitable Christian moment of Death and Transformation.

In October of 1986, Pope John Paul II invited representatives of all faiths to gather in Assisi to pray for peace on the feast of St. Francis. One hundred and sixty representatives of a dozen faiths were there. For a Church that has for centuries preached unambiguously that there is no salvation outside its walls, this was a major step toward spiritual harmony. To avoid seeming like the "president of presidents" the Pontiff caught a bus with other Christian representatives and quietly took his place at the rear of the procession through the town. (*Time Magazine*, November 10, 1986, p. 79)

We have endeavored to reduce the walls, to make good fences over which we can talk to our neighbors. Vatican Council II in 1963 initiated a dying process for outmoded forms which were nonessential. In many ways, the Catholic Church since 1963 has removed barriers and walls deliberately, and has worked toward greater understanding.

Why do I describe the Church in this transitional period? Because it is the time of greatest hope. The passage from death to life is the central meaning. Indeed, this is the central image in nature where the period of surrender seems to be easier, not so vehemently resisted; autumn and winter are recognized as crucial to spring and summer. For the institution to undergo its history of transformation is a sign of great hope. We eagerly await the new life. Who knows what the renewed life will be like?

What we do know is that Jesus Christ, the founder, knew His Jewish tradition well, and yet, He was required to move beyond the fence. In fact, He so scandalized his contempories that He was put to death beyond the walls.

Everyone of us will have to carry the cross of the Redeemer, not in the bright moments but in the darkest of times. As each one faces into the darkness, we may hope for the awakening of our own inner life. When the Christian life is *our* life, we will be moved through love for the poor and oppressed to take our place with those who don't belong, who are rejected by power because we are regarded as weak.

We share this challenge with other religions. It strikes me that the fence of tolerance is transitional. We will meet outside the walls; we will meet on our way up the mountain; we will meet in the search for our deepest roots in God. This does not imply a religious consensus as a negotiation of our faith convictions. Rather, it acknowledges that we all draw from the deepest and most life-giving sources and that we share everyone's concern for the future of humanity.

We are living between the ages, neither
in the old world nor yet in the new.

21

What Does It Mean
to Belong?

Harry M. Buck

In the church that I attended as a child we often sang John Greenleaf
Whittier's hymn, containing these words

New occasions teach new duties.
Time makes ancient good uncouth.
They must upward still and onward
Who would keep abreast of truth.

and the words of that poem have resonated through my mind in all
the years since.

But which way is upward? Which direction is onward? Have we
really entered a new era? If so, what redefinitions are called for?

I prefer to think that we are living between ages, neither in the
old world nor yet in the new. In our journey we are standing a bit as
Isaac did when his father Abraham had brought him to a foreign
land and then forbade marriage with any of the daughters of the
new land and also forbade him to return home.

In the Genesis story, Abraham had already tried to kill his son in
response to what he believed to be the command of God, and by

this time, Isaac's mother had died. A servant was dispatched to the home land to find a wife for Isaac and bring her back.

We know very little about the woman he found, for all stories about her were composed in a strongly patriarchal culture. We know only that with very little information and no real assurance, Rebekah said simply to Abraham's servant, "I will go." With this simple acceptance she left her family and her world to cross the desert and join a husband she had not yet met. What courage she must have had.

We also learn from the story that for whatever reason she favored her husband's younger son Jacob over his older brother Esau, even to the point of deceiving the old man, thereby changing the course of history.

How, then, can this story speak to our own existence? Rebekah and Isaac lived between the ages. Isaac did not strike out for a new existence as did his father Abraham — or Moses, or Jesus, or Gautama. He was not the formulator of a new tradition as was his son Jacob — or Muhammad or Gandhi. Yet Isaac and his resourceful wife Rebekah provided a link between the old age that had been left behind and the new age that was dawning.

I

In the Age of Isaac in which we must live at the end of the twentieth century, we have come to realize that the answers to questions that gave us such comfort as children no longer suffice. But we do not have new ones firmly entrenched to take their place. Indeed, few of us want to give up the past, for the heritage is precious.

In the first several essays of this volume we came face to face with concerns about the integrity of past traditions and the institutions supporting them. Here we encountered not simply religious tradition but "religions" in the strictest sense of the word.

Few forces in the world are more divisive than language and religion, and the two identities are frequently intertwined. Italian, German, Latin, Hebrew, Arabic, Tamil, Punjabi, Sinhalese, and so on designate not only languages spoken by various groups of people; they roughly define religious boundaries as well. Language and religion both have to do with ways of thinking, with one's view of the world and what is important about it.

What separates persons who speak different languages — particularly when these languages are from radically different sources — is not a simple matter of vocabulary; it is frequently an expression of entire value systems. The same is true of what we call religion or its plural *religions*. They are not just different modes of worship or variations in doctrine. R eligions, then, will by nature, be conservative. It is a creative minority in any religious system — be it Hindu, Buddhist, Sikh, Jewish, Muslim, or Christian — that has a broad social vision that is world-wide and not confined within its own boundaries.

For this reason, among others, the word *religion* has no adequate definition, and it is significant that in the languages of India and many other Asian languages, a word for *religion* simply doesn't exist. When discussing religion in this context we must abandon the notion of religion as a collection of beliefs. To ask "What does a Hindu believe?" "What does a Sikh believe?" "What does a Muslim or a Jew or a Christian believe?" will not convey an adequate grasp of reality. Much more is at stake.

Sometimes we speak of "organized religion." Religion is by definition organized. Thus, when we talk about religion in the sense of its institutions we are not talking about individual spiritual experience. That's something else, and it can happen outside a temple, mosque, or church as readily as inside it, and a few years ago many voices said more readily outside than inside. Religions, then, as one author has put it are "extremely dangerous animals."[1] When used as the legitimators of power plays, they have even been called "licensed insanities."

On occasion religions will sanction violence, killing in order to glorify God and protect "His" religion. Even a religious system as peace-minded as Theravāda Buddhism has a scripture that tells the story of King Dutthagamani ca 100 BCE1 who had second thoughts about the extensive massacres he had performed on behalf of Buddhism. But he was told by the bhikkhus monks1 that he had brought glory to the Buddha, and that since those killed were not believers, they did not merit the respect he would have given them had they

---

1. J. W. Bowker, "the Burning Fuse: The Unacceptable Face of Religion." *Zygon*, 21/4 (December 1986), pp. 415ff.

been truly human.[2] The great Mahatma, Gandhi, stressed non-violence, but he did so while appealing to a book, the *Bhagavad Gita*, which urges Arjuna to fight, even though it means killing his loved ones in defense of his dharma. Gandhiji himself was assassinated by devout Hindus, even as his successor Indira was not shot down by her Sikh bodyguards — all in the name of religions that preach world peace and harmony. Religions, then, do accept violence in defense of the faith.

On the other hand, "organized religion" has been one of the most important creative impulses in the world.

II

The second group of essays saw a more subtle distinction. Here we saw religion not as a set of institutions to be defended but as a series of communities in which persons interact with each other, share common values, and develop distinctive ways of life. One generally "belongs" to a group, a church, a synagogue, a sangha, a community of some sort, and these communities define themselves in varying terms with quite different degrees of toleration or acceptance or intercommunion.

In this context persons may speak a distinctive language, frequently dress in an identifiable manner and have very little contact with those of other communities, although they may live in the same neighborhood. There is a quite natural tendency for people who share the same values, speak the same language, worship at the same shrines, to want to live together with outsiders excluded. Only then, so some think, can we live out our beliefs to full measure. Sister Joan Kirby's characterization of walls and fences speaks eloquently to this point.

Recent years have witnessed growing strength and vitality among religious communities demanding rigid adherance to belief or practice, developing a fortress mentality about their own turf, excluding, denouncing, and condemning those of us who do not belong, who cannot participate in their way of life. At the same time there has never been an age when more men and women were concerned deeply about the common bond of humanity that unites us

2. From the *Mahavamsa*, 25:101ff., quoted in Bowker, p. 425.

— and unites us in those profound depths of our spirituality where labels of possession no longer matter, where belonging takes on a different meaning.

Yet, there remains a dilemma for many of us who would like to participate — to participate fully, to "belong" — in many different contexts; but who cannot give supreme loyalty to any one of them. Worship belongs to something more fundamental than any society or any religion. What does it mean to belong?

That ubiquitous authority, the dictionary, gives me four definitions of "belong." I can say "My pen belongs in my pocket" — an orderly way of finding a place for everything and putting everything in its place. If I say, "This pen belongs to me," however, I have asserted ownership; you may not write with it unless you have my permission. If I use my pen to write a book about religion, a librarian will say it belongs in the 200 section of the Dewey Decimal System or in the B section of the Library of Congress system. A library book or a computer file can belong only in one place, and we like to classify men and women the same way. It's convenient, like putting a dog's name on his collar if you don't want him to get lost. But it's phony. The dog isn't really Fido; I am not Harry Buck; both these names were given by someone who is not a dog and someone who is not me. These labels do not convey that unique set of experiences that is me.

III

Another dictionary-sanctioned usage, which may lead us to the final collection of essays in this volume, celebrating the primacy of human experience, is to say something like "Pen and paper belong together," thus asserting relationship. This comes closer, because I believe that the real meaning of belong is to love, to live, and to learn, to eat of the tree of life more than of the tree of judgment, to participate fully in the Ultimate Reality of all there is — and by whatever human means there are.

In the early chapters of Genesis there is a reference to trees. Trees with their concentric growth rings, rooted in the earth with leafy branches stretching heavenward. Two trees at the center of a garden from which we have expelled ourselves, the tree of life and the tree of discrimination [knowledge of good and evil]. We need the fruit of the tree of discrimination, else we should know very little in our age. But when we preferred this tree to the tree of life, which is the true *axis mundi*, we became judgmental and discriminatory. Right now we need more than anything else to eat of the tree of life.

Despite the fact that few forces are as divisive as religion, one may still hope that because I am human no human tradition is alien to me. And I believe it is a wrong exegesis of Darwin to assume that survival of the fittest means the survival of the toughest and the most exclusive; it means, and always has meant, the survival of those best fitted to the demands of the times. Right now that demand is exactly the opposite of greater armaments and ideological loyalties.

To live, to love, to learn — to participate fully without exclusive loyalties. That is the kind of belonging we need today. It can be found in the contemplative life in which spirit transcends label and experience supersedes judgment.

Each of these three groups of essays has sounded important notes. Human life is lived in community, and communities demand organizations. But their needs change, and so must we. Can we find the courage of Rebekah and the strength of Isaac?

Contributors

Louis J. Hammann is Professor of Religion and Chair of Interdepartmental Studies at Gettysburg College. He teaches and writes in the area of world religions with emphases on Near Eastern and Asian religions.

Harry M. Buck is a founder of the American Academy of Religion and was managing editor of its journal for 16 years. He has taught History of Religion at Wellesley and Wilson Colleges.

Michael J. McTighe is Assistant Professor of Religion at Gettysburg College. He specializes in religion in the United States and nineteenth century social history.

Sheikh Mubarak Ahmad is presently serving as the Chief Missionary of the Ahmadiyya Movement in Islam, with its National Headquarters at Washington, D.C. and its missions spread throughout North America.

John Borelli is the Executive Secretary, Secretariat for Interreligious Relations, National Conference of Catholic Bishops located in Washington, D.C. He has also served as the Secretary-General/USA for the World Conference on Religion and Peace, a multireligious non-governmental organization affiliated with the United Nations.

Anita Ioas Chapman is of a third generation American Baha'i family. She currently works with the Baha'i Office of External Affairs in Washington, D.C.

Robert Jules Chaumont is the Center Director of the Unification Church in Towson, Maryland. He was graduated from the Unification Theological Seminary in Barrytown, New York in 1985.

Donald Freeman is Professor of Theology and Ministry and Director of Doctoral Stuides at the Lancaster Theological Seminary.

Paul D. Gehris is with the Pennsylvania Council of Churches and serves as both the Director of its Office of Social Ministry and the Coordinator of Pennsylvania IMPACT. He has a Doctor of Ministry from the Lancaster Theological Seminary and has served as pastor of several Baptist churches in Pennsylvania.

Steven J. Gelberg/Subhananda dās is currently studying comparative religion and Hindu studies at Harvard Divinity School. He continues to publish the *ISKCON Review* and is a resource person for scholars and students doing ISKCON — related research.

Helen Glassman is a senior student and monk at the Zen Community of New York in Yonkers. She is a student of Bernard Tetsugen Glassman Sensei and manager of the community's bakery which is their livelihood practice and social action practice.

Naomi R. Goldenberg is Associate Professor of the Psychology of Religion at the University of Ottawa, where she is writing about psychoanalysis and feminism.

Scott W. Gustafson is Assistant Professor of Systematic Theology at the Lutheran Theological Seminary in Gettysburg, Pennsylvania. He has served as the pastor of Lutheran Churches in Virginia and Maryland.

Sister Joan Kirby is a religious of the Sacred Heart. She is the Executive Director of Homes For the Homeless, an Interfaith Project of the Cathedral of Saint John the Divine in New York City.

Anne Myers formerly a member of the Southern Baptist Church, is currently an ordained minister in the Presbyterian Church U.S.A. She is pastor of the Great Conowago Presbyterian Church in Hunterstown, Pennsylvania.

Robert Paul is Associate Professor of History of Science at Dickinson College. He serves as a lay minister in the Mormon Church.

Stanley Ned Rosenbaum is Associate Professor of Classics and Religion at Dickinson College. His speciality is Judaic studies.

Uma A. Saini is an ordained minister of the Hindu faith and has been teaching Hindi at the American University, Washington, D.C., for the past fifteen years. Prior to coming to the United States she taught Sanskrit language and literature at the Janaki Devi College in Delhi and the Agra College, Agra, India.

Edward Stoltzfus is Associate Professor of Theology at the Seminary at Eastern Mennonite College.

K.R. Sundararajan is Chairman of the Theology Department at St. Bonaventure University, New York. He was graduated from the University of Madras and has taught at Punjabi University, Patiala, India.

Charles Teague is Pastor of the Country and Town Baptist Church in Mechanicsburg, Pennsylvania. He holds degrees from Cornell Law School and the Southern Baptist Theological Seminary.

Anthony Ugolnik, an Associate Professor of English at Franklin and Marshall College, is an ethnic Russian who is ordained as a deacon in the Greek Orthodox Church.